Badassery 101

Ten Secrets to Be the Confident Boss of Your Life

By
Roseanney Liu

Also by Roseanney Liu

You did WHAT now?! (2017)
How to Survive Elementary School (2017)
Mastering Your Inner Game (2018)
Phenomenal Women (2018)

Scorpius Media LLC
Redondo Beach, California 90277
www.Roseanney .com

First published in the United States of America by Scorpius Media,
2018.

ISBN 9780998334448 (paperback)

THE LIBRARY OF CONGRESS HAS CATALOGED THE
PAPERBACK EDITION AS FOLLOWS:

Name: Liu, Roseanney, 1977- author.
Title: Badassery 101: Ten secrets to being the confident boss of your
 life / Roseanney Liu.
Description: Los Angeles: Scorpius Media, 2018.

Identifiers: LCCN 2018906007 (print)
Subjects: Self-actualization (Psychology) Self-help techniques.
BISAC: SELF-HELP / Motivational & Inspirational.
SELF-HELP / Personal Growth / General

Book Interior and Ebook design by Amit Dey

LC record available at https://lccn.loc.gov/2018906007

Table of Contents

Introduction

Did you miss the memo?

You know, the one about you being the confident, badass boss of your life?

Yeah, that one.

Well, in case you missed it, here it is again:

July 2018

Dear Friend,

YOU ARE THE CONFIDENT BADASS BOSS OF YOUR LIFE. You already have what it takes to live like a badass, within legitimate and legal means, and do everything you want to do in life.

So act like it.

Sincerely,
Roseanney Liu

Oh, but how? My parents won't let me. My partner won't let me. My ex-so and so won't let me. But, but,

but...I'm too scared! I don't know how! I don't know where to begin to live like the boss of my life. Or, maybe this sounds like you: *I'm so used to being told what to do and when to do it. I'm being pulled in so many other directions. I don't know how to take control.*

But but but!

Please snap out of it. Now.

You picked up this book because either you know me or you liked the cover, or you liked the book description, or you've been to one of my talks and know I'm an action taker and what I say will get your bottom into gear too.

I've been in your shoes before where Fear and Doubt and other people's shit hit against my own inner badassery and dimmed it for a second to a couple of years. My life experiences where my confidence was put to the test have been, and not limited to:

- Stigma & limitations against children who come from divorced parents (mine called it quits when I was 9).
- Facing challenges as an immigrant when I was 11
- Naysayers, even when they see I'm on my way or have already done some cool shit
- Switching career gears so many times I've lost count (to finally finding what I'm meant to do for and in this world)

- Criticism – constructive as well as ill-intentioned ones
- Climbing mountains – sometimes not sure if I could make it to the summit or hike down to the trailhead safely

But I have learned and gotten reacquainted with my badassery, my inner confidence – the one that enables me to move forward and live the best life as the best version of myself. I can now call my badassery to me on command when Fear and Doubt rear their ugly heads again so that I can forge forward on my amazing path.

I want you to feel that you CAN and WILL do the same.

So here's the gist: In this book I'm giving you ten secrets with action steps on how to implement each to live like the unapologetic, awesome, strong badass boss of your life that you are meant to be. No one can act like this high-level boss in your life as you can, and you will know exactly how to do so as you read this book.

You will know how to tap into that inner confidence you were born with; the confidence that perhaps got muted in one shape or another because life experiences or societal norms told you to turn the volume down, directly or indirectly. Well, you are going to learn how to unmute that *Confidence* button and turn the volume up, way up again, and live as the confident boss of your life.

You are going to learn what to do to live the life you want to live, do the things you want to do even when the goals seem gargantuan and insurmountable. You are going to pursue the things you want, each and every time, consistently.

You are going to learn how self-validation is the best validation and it's the eternal fountain of awesomeness which you already possess. This and several other concepts and implementation steps will help you live like a total badass.

Easy peasy.

Let's dive in. And, welcome to the Badassery 101 Club.

Roseanney

Download the freebie PDF today from my website and get 3 tips on how to start unleashing your badassery today.

Use this link and scroll to the bottom of the webpage:

www.Roseanney.com

1

Figure out how to do the hard shit and then do it

a. Observe role models

b. Reverse engineer

c. Tell people what you are up to – help will manifest

To accomplish great things, we must not only act but also dream, not only plan but also believe.

— Anatole France

Nothing that's worth doing comes easily.

— President Theodore Roosevelt

Note that they did *not* say, "So don't do anything that seems hard."

To be human and deserve our place at the apex of the food chain, we are conditioned to do this very thing: Figure out how to problem-solve and just do it.

Do you think cavemen just gave up the first 100 times they couldn't make fire given a couple of rocks and sticks while sitting at dusk? No. They kept on trying until they lit a fire and then *aha!* – warmth and cooked meat!

Do you think mountains are just placed on earth to be admired from afar? No. If they were, tens of thousands of climbers and hikers couldn't say they have summited Kilimanjaro or Denali or Everest Base Camp or any other high altitude mountains that are gorgeous and daunting.

Here's the thing and it might come as a news flash: Everything beyond sitting on your couch and binge-watching *The Bachelor* is hard.

Sometimes it's hard to make social plans with friends and show up (especially when you have kids). But you do it – because maintaining any kind of relationship and connection takes effort.

A lot of times in a new business endeavor you don't know what you are doing, especially if you are scared shitless to take action because the fear of making mistakes that cost time and money is a real deterrent. I know, I've been there. But it didn't stop me from doing a lot of research, doing some reverse engineering, asking questions, and taking a whole lot of other action steps before publishing two books simultaneously and delivering both to Amazon's best-selling status in 2017.

Sometimes it's hard to have difficult conversations with people – people you love, people who are strangers or acquaintances. But you don't know what's in their heads or what they are dealing with – you only know what's in *your* head – until you have that conversation. Having the conversation is step #1 to moving a stagnant situation forward. Progressing forward is key and I'll talk about this in more detail in chapters six and seven.

So, in short, many things are hard. But it doesn't mean we should just not try. In fact, quite the opposite.

Here's what happens when you attempt to do the hard shit with something you want in life:

> Your brain will hurt and you will feel stressed – your brain will be like, *what is this gosh darn exercise you are putting me through?! I was perfectly happy sitting here as a mush watching* The Bachelor! Your brain will whine a lot and try to hurt you by producing headaches. But then…

> Your brain will start to get excited, because its cells and neurons will be stimulated as they travel on a mental journey they've never been on before. Everything seems new and scary, yet exciting to them. They are happy and nervous and a little afraid at what they

might experience around the corner. This, in turn, makes your brain happy. This is what makes you excited. Your brain starts exercising muscles it didn't even know it had and it becomes giddy and wants more! For each neuron connecting and expanding, the brain becomes stronger. *You* become stronger and more knowledgeable about a problem or a program that is a mystery, at first, until you start to decode it. Each connection makes the unknown path a little more lit and solid. Before you know it, your brain becomes braver and knocks on doors for you to expand on this new work; the brain starts connecting the dots on its own to ask the questions that should be asked. And it goes to places and people that would probably know the answers.

The brain becomes more thirsty as you keep on feeding it from the fountain of knowledge to solve a problem. The brain knows that only by staying *hydrated* with information – and by acting on that information – can it get into better shape. Your brain wants to be in better shape since it now sees and feels what the exercise is doing. It is getting more muscular, stronger, faster, happier. It wants more from the fountain. It wants more problems to solve because it knows it is capable and you are the vehicle to provide the tool kit to help it solve problems. It demands the hard shit because, after all, it is a human brain; doing hard shit is what it was born to do before laziness and contentedness masked that preternatural condition. Besides, the brain knows it isn't one big hard climb to the top for whatever you want to do; it knows that each little attempt is a stepping stone that yields knowledge or rewards driving you to accomplish the next goal.

Many of your goals seem hard – such as starting a new business with which you have zero experience. Getting that four-year degree. Getting a foot in the door of the place where you want to work or have an apprenticeship. Heck, even going on vacation to your dream destination may seem difficult due to financial restrictions or mindset limitations on how to navigate once you are there.

But, you can still tackle the hard stuff and have forward progression in order to make your brain and your soul happy. It will bitch and moan at first, believe me. Here's how you do it:

a. Observe the role models

b. Reverse engineer

c. Tell people what you are up to... help will manifest

Observe the role models

How do you even know if you want something? Usually, by sheer imagination or by seeing someone else obtaining or achieving that goal. You feel a little pull that indicates *I want that.*

Here's an example: I have never heard of an author publishing two books at the same time but I set out to do exactly that in the spring of 2017. I imagined it happening. I knew many authors who were prolific in terms of publishing books in their genre: Seth Godin and his umpteen million books (ok, dozens). Another prolific author that everyone has heard of is John Grisham. Plus, there was that guy Robert in one of my writers' groups who'd written and published eight books on coaching and mindset. I have seen many others who had obtained or achieved a similar goal, so it wasn't a stretch for me to imagine that publishing more than one book at a time is possible.

Imagination tells you what's possible.

What you see manifesting as a reality for others tells you what's possible AND practical.

So, besides sheer imagination – which is a thing of beauty and provides the faucet for the fountain knowledge in your brain – you seek out role models that are doing or have done what you want to do.

You look at what they are doing and how they are doing it:

How they are branding themselves – what's their story

What vehicle(s) they are using to achieve what they are doing – *what kind of online and offline presence are they utilizing*

What kinds of people are part of their "team"

What technical tools they are using

One of the best selling nonfiction authors I follow, Jeff Goins, touts himself as a successful blogger/author who came up from nothing with no audience who wanted to share his knowledge that there's artistry and money behind the craft of writing if one just knows how to utilize some tools. This is his branding story and part of his expertise. Jeff is active on his Facebook page, and he blogs and emails his list regularly. All of this is how he stays engaged with his audience and maintains his message via his online presence. He also has an annual Tribe conference at which he connects with other artists of all sorts of media to inspire and to motivate conference participants. This is his offline presence. Jeff has built his empire and following to the degree that he has a marketing team, including a literary agent and publisher, that runs his conference bookings, speaking engagements, and regular production of his social media posts. Did he start at this level? Of course not. He built it step by step, like anybody and everybody else who reaches that level.

While Jeff is a writer role model for me, I gleaned from observing him that there is merit to a blog that consistently has useful info for the subscribers and fans. But that's not something I want to deploy as part of audience engagement. Instead, I'll use a blog to post articles about what I experience and observe in life (the fountain for my nonfiction works) as well as in-depth looks at where I am and what I'm learning about publishing my next books. My blog might include snippets from *A Crazy Day on the Job As a...* a nonfiction collection of humor and career advice stories that I set to publish in 2019. *Crush Your Teen Years* is a graphic novel depicting situations and advice for teens on how to deal with issues that come up during teenhood years and I might include in my blog interesting findings that come up as I interview teens and education professionals for this book.

Another best selling fiction and nonfiction author I follow is UK-based Joanna Penn who not only publishes successfully across genres, she also offers helpful products like a blog, e-books, webinars and courses teaching newer authors how to market books and write productively. She has podcasts showcasing her wisdom as well as interviews with other experts in publishing posted on her website and Facebook page. Joanna also talks with other publishing experts so they can share more pearls of wisdom for her followers. She does all of that while continuing to write her books.

What I learn from Joanna is that while she's incredibly multi-talented and provides a tremendous amount of useful content for writers, I'm interested in doing only a fraction of what she does. I present curated content on what I learn by publishing Facebook live video format (so podcasting is out for me, at least for now). My targeted audience and curated content are for nonfiction authors only.

A ton of people – A TON – want to travel the world while running an online business that gives them financial freedpm and supports their lifestyle. There are just as many people already doing this and some of them *teach you how to do it.* So if you truly want to achieve this goal, you don't ask *How* can I? You ask, *How can I not?* and *Why not me?!*

When the student is ready, the teacher appears. The way forward is to look at role models and glean information on what seems to be working for them. Pick which parts you want to emulate and incorporate into your own goals. As long as the strategies and tactics make sense for your goals and mission, go ahead and deploy them. The learning process unfolds as you implement strategies that will enable you to live like the badass you are.

Reverse Engineer

As I wrote before, everything new seems exciting or scary or difficult.

But there's a logical progression of how to achieve your goal, whether it's your general badassery, a new skill, or reaching best selling rank on Amazon or in the *New York Times*.

Or whatever the heck you want to do.

Here's how to do the thing you really *want* to do:

Let's start with the "easy" stuff. Let's say you need to figure out whether to go to that new networking event or a party where you don't know anyone. Apply the five-second rule as touted by Mel Robbins; the thing you *want* to do may be much harder than the thing you *need* to do. (complete that project with a looming deadline), but the same tactic applies – think for 5 seconds the pros and cons and how your mental, physical and emotional and spiritual health will be as a result of doing this thing. If the result will be overwhelmingly positive and outweighs the cons (the effort) of doing it, then just fucking do it!

Your five seconds are up. It's time to do or die. Well, not that extreme. But you get my point.

The thing you want to do may be as simple as taking a 30-minute walk each morning because you know it's good for you. You would enjoy it but you need to find the time to do it. By the way, I firmly believe you either make time for something or you make excuses, but you cannot make both at the same time. This applies to something as difficult as having a hard conversation with a family member or a client or climbing Mt Everest. If your mind keeps coming back to one thing, it's trying to tell you that it really needs to be done. Something in your heart or your soul needs it and craves it. It may be that the next thing cannot come to fruition until you accomplish this thing, so to speak.

In February, 2017 I started thinking about an outdoor physical activity that I wanted to take on and do regularly. Which one did I like best and want to improve in terms of skills? Canoe racing was out; I'd been there, done that and hated the way it taxed my body by working against the ocean and the oars. Biking wasn't really my thing either, although I enjoy leisure biking. So I decided on hiking. It wasn't long before I fell in love with the movement of hiking and viewing incredible scenery. I picked up more gear and clothing from REI because I wanted to look legit and be prepared – a backpack, water bladder, trekking poles and good quality hiking boots were added. I began thinking about how I could hike even higher altitudes and what challenges in the local geography other hikers usually gave themselves. That segued into the Six Peak Challenge of Southern California – mountain summits ranging from 8,000 feet to 11,500 feet in elevation. As I was knocking down each of the first five peaks over the spring and summer, another question and goal emerged: What well known peak from another state or continent could I reasonably attempt with only a few months of hiking experience?

Mt Kilimanjaro immediately sprang to mind. Don't ask me why.

With zero long distance or high altitude hiking experience before February, 2017, I summited one peak after another. They were almost in ascending order in terms of peak altitudes in southern California. Summiting mountains is the literal definition of overcoming hardships to accomplish a singular goal. It added so much badassery to my soul. For me, climbing mountains was not only great exercise, it was a confidence booster. It mirrored writing and publishing books from the standpoint of not having any experience in that either! The process of doing something new and giving myself permission to try hard and move forward were a *massive confidence booster.*

So, how does one get from A to Z? How does one go from zero long distance or high altitude hiking experience to one of the holy grails of being on Kilimanjaro? How does anyone go from having no experience to achieving a goal for which one's soul calls?

Reverse engineer it.

Obviously I couldn't and didn't go from walking on surface streets at nearly sea level to the second highest point of Kilimanjaro at 18,400 feet. I had to train for it, in distance and in altitude.

I began with short local hikes such as the trails by the ocean in Rancho Palos Verdes, Southern California. Trails are mostly easy to moderate, can be completed up and back in three to four hours and the altitude is 1,000 feet, at most.

When I heard about the Six-Peak Challenge of SoCal. I realized this could a good little training starter pack, if you will, for the holy grail of Kilimanjaro. I also heard about Mt Whitney; 14,505 feet in altitude, the 11th highest peak in the U.S. and THE highest mountain summit in the contiguous U.S. So, while I did shorter hikes here and there between where I live in the South Bay beach cities to Santa Clarita Valley and Hollywood, I also joined groups of people who were tackling the six peaks. Between June and September 2017, I completed five of the six peaks that ranged 8,000 feet to 10,500 feet before flying to Tanzania in late September to attempt Kilimanjaro over a six-day hiking trip.

I learned from my mistakes, such as the error of doing Mt Baldy first (10,080 feet elevation), the one with the steepest elevation increase in the first two hours. I did not follow suggestions in the hiking articles that offered starting with Mt Wilson at 5,713 feet elevation. I learned that high quality hiking boots and in-soles will help curb extraordinarily sore feet. Yep, I learned the hard way.

Overall, I learned that my hiking badassery had to be gained incrementally by following good advice from others who had come before me on those peaks. I learned to climb per ascending altitude order, also called elevation difficulty order. I learned to always pack more than enough water, sustenance and a map. Otherwise, the badass mountains would always win and teach me certain lessons the hard way.

So how will you reverse engineer the process to achieve your goal?

By figuring out the following:

- What is the big goal, the big get? For me in terms of publishing, it was reaching Amazon Best Seller rank for my books.

- What needs to come right before your big goal? For me, it was gaining a huge amount of buyers in a particular book category on Amazon in any given hour on launch day.
- What needs to come right before that last mini-goal? For me, it was figuring out when the most friends and fans were most accessible online, and posting about my books at the optimal times.
- What needs to come right before that last mini-goal? For me, it was figuring out which ways are the best in reaching friends and fans on launch day via Facebook posts, Twitter posts, direct emails the day before or two days before.
- What needs to come right before that last mini-goal? For me, it was finding out how to tell people that I was coming out with two books on the same day. Each time I was interviewed by the media, I learned to post the pictures with the interview in my own social media and include the launch date to cement it into my followers' minds.
- What needs to come right before that last mini-goal?(find media to interview me about the books via my contacts and my friends' contacts – do this as much in advance as

possible because, hello? Media's schedules do not revolve around my book launch so I'd need to give them as much notice as possible to provide me the space to be interviewed. And, the right pitch is key!)

- What needs to come right before that last mini-goal? For me, it was finding out what kinds of media would be interested in interviewing me, and pinpointing how my books would serve their audience.

As you see, two patterns emerge:

- Each goal is preceded by another one, a smaller, more digestible one, because we simply do not go from 0 to 100 mph in two seconds. Well, give Tesla a couple more years and maybe we will see a vehicle that can actually do that. Each mini-goal is exact and serves as a stepping stone to the goal right after it. Brainstorming, talking with people or masterminding in groups – both inside and outside of your industry - will help you uncover that series of action steps or stepping stones that you need to walk on to help you achieve the huge, final goal.

- Each preceding goal is smaller and more doable than the one following it, so obviously a brainstorming process made me see that one of my first steps was to find out what kinds of media would like to interview me and get to know my books based on the audience they serve, and that first goal is a hell of a lot more digestible and doable than the end-goal of "reaching best selling rank on Amazon".

When you do this reverse engineering process, you will calm down your mind from the freak-out and the self-doubt and the fear of *"No I cannot do this"*, because you are mapping out a plan of action steps that you can do one at a time, even one day at time, that will put you on the right course to achieving something big you want.

Go on now: Get your laptop out or go old school and get out a pen and paper and write out the reverse engineered steps to achieving something you want to do and start living your life like a confident badass. When you are not sure – and there will be times when you are not sure what the preceding steps would be – you will do research and/or join masterminds and/or ask your friends (the "right" friends and people in your networks, by the way, more about that in chapter 3) and believe me, you WILL uncover the steps. Knowledge simply shows itself to inquiring minds.

I am cheering you on the sidelines through the growing pains and the joys of you doing the hard shit and eventually, achieving what you set out to do. I'll be ready to toast you with champagne when you get there.

Tell people what you are up to... help will manifest

Part of embracing badassery is being unapologetic and fearless. Tell people what you want. Say aloud what you are up to, because nobody lives in your head. It's a great talent to be telepathic, but most of us simply do not have it. Even if you don't know HOW to get to your goal yet, tell the world what it is you want.

Do you want to travel the world on a budget? Say so, and tell everyone.

Do you want to change the curriculum of your class, of your school district, of your state and you have a game plan? Say so, and tell everyone.

Do you want to teach kids photography because you think it's a cool art form and you know many kids will flourish with this art form? Say so, and tell everyone!

The point is, it is your duty to be your own #1 fan and biggest advocate. You owe it to yourself to say aloud what you want and what you are trying to achieve and to do it repeatedly to anyone who will listen. What happens after you say what you want aloud is magic: the right people who can and want to help you will show up in your life out of the blue because the Universe listens; the opportunities for you to align yourself toward your dream goals start popping up because the Universe is paving stepping stones for you; the learning curve and the toolkit you should have become clearer because you should have whatever it takes to achieve.

The first time I said aloud that I would love to climb Kilimanjaro was August, 2016 when I visited my friend, Nyambura and her family in Seattle with my little boy in tow. I just blurted it aloud to her, and that was even before I started hiking seriously. She happened to mention that her sister Reachel, based in Switzerland, was training to climb the same mountain. My friend said, "You should talk to my sister and pick her brain about the training."

I didn't think too much of it then because I wasn't seriously hiking at that time. It seemed like a pipe dream to climb Kilimanjaro with all its 19,341 feet of altitude majesty and then do a safari afterwards to take in the Serengeti.

Then, I started getting into hiking more, and the distance of my hikes got longer and the altitude more intensive. Kilimanjaro did not seem just a pipe dream after all.

I talked about it in private with Nyamburra, who told me that besides her sister Reachel, I should also connect with her childhood friend Maurice, a fellow Kenyan who now lived in Los Angeles. Maurice led hikes on Kilimanjaro a number of times while serving as a group photographer.

You'd better believe while I was training that I reached out to both Reachel and Maurice to ask them all about hiking on Mt Kili (as the natives affectionately call Kilimanjaro).

When you put your intentions out there, magic happens. The right people and opportunities somehow emerge.

Lately, what's been on my mind has been teens and their problems which are, in fact, also parents' and society's problems. My kids are not teens yet and do not nearly experience any issues that teens tend to face in today's world, but inexplicably, teen stuff has been weighing on my mind, not the least of which that teens have said so during panel discussions that I have attended in my community as well as issues dramatized on Netflix's *13 Reasons Why*. The problems they deal with – and I believe no teen is problem-free – range widely. Cyber-bullying, depressive and suicidal thoughts, self-medicating with alcohol and marijuana due to overwhelming pressure, worries about performing in classes and on the sports field, diminishing what they really want for themselves in order to fulfill parents' and teachers' aspirations for them, unwanted sexual advances and assaults... the list goes on and on.

When I was a teen, I also felt some pressure to perform my absolute best. I had tunnel vision about attending a four-year college and I also felt good about my backup plans if I did not attend any of the six colleges to which I had admission offers. But, I definitely did not have the host of other problems that I see many of today's teens face that stem from overwhelming access to screen time, social media and access to drugs and alcohol. Nobody pressured me to do anything but be the best student I could be. I had a close set of a few friends with whom I got along great and who were my support network throughout my high school years. Quite honestly, what today's teens need to deal with troubles and astounds me, including gun-related violence on campus, such as what took place at Columbine, Virginia Tech and at Marjory Stoneman Douglas High.

In January, 2018 the ideas of a new book and a teen summit started bubbling up in my mind. The book idea is about a Marvel style graphic novel crossed with a *Chicken Soup for the Teenage Soul* book that would serve as an advice book for teens on how to identify and work through issues. It would include resources on where to get additional help. Several literary agents told me it was a great and fascinating idea. One told me to spin it as more of an advice handbook for parents to make it more marketable. I also started sharing more about it on social media and in the community when I'm at networking events. I have stated that I'd like to give talks and workshops to teens so they can be empowered on a self-directed path, and live authentically despite all the challenges they face. I started telling people that I would like to organize a summit for teens and young adults wherein in one day they would attend a number of workshops and talks given by me and experts in other domains that teach the audience, essentially, how to do life – a life hack summit, as it were.

When I started talking and sharing about the book and the summit ideas, would you believe that in one week I had face to face contact with three other people also on this path of helping teens? They all wanted to work with me on bringing the talk and workshops to students. Since then, I have been working on talking with schools and sponsors about making this summit a reality as well as taking on more active role on the parents advisory board of a local nonprofit that is developing social/emotional wellness programs for teens. The circle of interconnectivity is continuing on its path and I'm positive with like-minded people in the community, we are going to spearhead great programs and eventually, my idea of the life hack summit for the adolescents.

I had put it out there that this was something I wanted to strive for – to be of service in my community to the teen market. My vehicles are a book and a talk/workshop/summit which I can offer to be of service to this market. Almost serendipitously, I connected with people on the same vibrational path.

But first, I had to say my intentions aloud. I had to say it to anyone who would listen.

See, if nobody knows who you are and what you want to do, NOTHING happens.

But you picked up this book, because you wanted SOMETHING to happen. You are ready for either a change or the next step.

Please let me repeat as we round out this chapter, "Say what you want aloud, say it often, say it to anyone who will listen, and the Universe will provide."

2

Be Your Own #1 Fan;
how to deal with critics

You can't let praise or criticism get to you.
It's a weakness to get caught up in either one.

— John Wooden

No one can give you validation better than or more than yourself.

For as long as you are alive, your intrinsic fountain of self-validation runs on tap; it runs from an eternal spring sourced from the mountain of greatness that is uniquely you. No one can give you unlimited, *"You've got this"* or *"You are good enough"* other than… you guessed it – YOU!

Are you waiting for someone to act as the Monopoly Man and tell you to pass Go and collect $200? Is some individual or group outside yourself going to deem you good enough? When is that going to take place, exactly?

It is badass to give yourself the validation, the go-ahead, and the pat on the back because deep down inside, you already know you are good enough. It is badass to believe that you are ready to take the plunge into that next venture or project. It is badass to make an idea come to fruition by execution and taking actions. Even if you don't know how you're going to get it done, you might surprise yourself and rise to the occasion once you are in the thick of doing the thing you want to do.

Ultimately, I did not reach the Kilimanjaro summit at 19,341 feet in October, 2017. Frostbite was setting in and I did not want to lose my fingers in exchange for climbing another 1,000+ feet to summit. I certainly did not wait for anyone to tell me that I was ready to make that climb when I had six months of hiking experience under my belt. I simply told myself that I wanted to and that I was ready. In fact, I *was* ready, minus the almost-frostbite, which I now know can be prevented during my next summiting attempt in 2019 or 2020 on the same mountain.

Although I did not, and still do not, personally know any author who wrote and independently published two nonfiction books at the same time, I told myself that I was ready and pulled both nonfiction titles to Amazon best selling rank on their simultaneous release date in 2017. Again, nobody told me I could or could not do it. I did not consult anyone for their opinion on the likelihood of making that happen – I researched enough to know what had to be done for each book and did my work for both titles, at the same time.

When was the last time you waited to do something until you got the green light from someone else? When was the last time you waited for a milestone to take place because you believed the milestone stood between you and your goal? When was the last time you kept your actions small or nil because you didn't hear overwhelming validation from the people you deemed to be judges?

If you did wait and keep yourself small, WHY? Why did you give that power away? I ask, because that power to decide when you are good to go was already within you in the first place, yet you just gave it away. Why?

When was the last time you actually asked for a raise? When was the last time you volunteered to step into a position because you knew you could do it better than the current or former individual in that position?

What stopped you from doing so?

It's time to take that power back, my friend. The eternal fountain of self-validation is trickling and awaiting you to take a sip. Nothing feels more powerful and right than giving validation and a green light to yourself. The only person's permission you need to do something or to set out to achieve a goal is YOU. And no one will validate you unless you validate yourself first; you have to be the first one and the biggest supporter of yourself. Know that you are actually quite good at something – that you are ready.

So what will you allow yourself to do today, tomorrow and the next day?

Does it sound like any of the following?

- I give myself the time, energy and the follow-through to get a loan so my new business idea can get off the ground.

- I allow myself to get babysitter for a day so that I can practice self-care in a quiet space.

- I give myself props that I'm good at _____ because I give my clients the result of _____ and _____. Therefore, I will get more referrals as a result and build out my business.

- I give myself permission to go to an event by myself even though I don't know anyone there because I know I will make a good impression. I look forward to getting to know at least _____ (# of) people.

- I'm ready to travel to _____ (country) on my own because it's a bucket list of mine and I've done months of research and learned enough survival language phrases. ; I look forward to having the time of my life in this country as I travel by myself for two weeks.

- I will allow myself to ask for a specific leadership position in this organization even though I am kind of new because I know I have the skill set and energy to do a great job in that role.

Think about it. And write down a list of things you are starting to allow yourself to do right now. The only person's permission and validation you need has been, and still is, your own.

Drink from the fountain of self-validation for it is unlimited, it's always ready to serve you, and it's got your back.

How to deal with critics

Do you know what else is as certain as death and taxes? Criticism.

Whether it's from yourself or from others, criticism is as reliable as fear, always there in the corner trying to knock your self-esteem down a few notches. Unconstructive criticism is always stopping you from doing what your heart and soul desire.

Now that you know it's a certain thing that will show up in life no matter where you are or what you are doing, know how to deal with criticism by answering three questions:

- Who is the critic and is their expertise relevant to what I'm doing?
- What IS the criticism and how is it delivered?
- What is the intention behind the criticism? (would it help me or my audience or my family? Would it make anyone or anything better as a result?)

The only time you need to heed criticism is when you can honestly acknowledge the following to yourself:

The critic has walked in my path before. They have "been there, done that" and have the expertise or knowledge base to tell me that I'm off-path with what I'm doing. Maybe they know intimately someone else who has walked my path before so they have nearly a first-hand knowledge base that what I'm doing is not the best for me. Maybe the critic has expert knowledge in an area that's relevant or transferable to what I'm doing so I have reason to believe they know what they are talking about.

What the people say in their criticism and how they deliver it are also key. If you are level-headed and pretty thick-skinned, you can usually see that nine times out of ten they are saying something about your work, not about you personally. Are they trying to say your x-y-z can be improved in a certain area? Are you trying to see their point as a nonpartisan receiver of the x-y-z? Or are you sensitive about it? If they are not attacking your character but are simply stating a certain aspect of your thing that can be improved for you or for your audience/customer's benefit, listen up. Often, people get offended by the criticism and fail to see that the other person's perceptions are also true and that what we do has a correlation to how someone else might perceive it; we cannot control how they perceive it, but we have control over how we influence the perception. So if someone tells you there's something well within your control that you can change in order to increase the positive perception from a certain audience, why wouldn't you listen closely?

Lastly, gauge what the critic's intention is. Do you believe that they have your best interest at heart? Why is that? Do you see that they have tried helping others with similar feedback? Have they celebrated your past successes and tried to lift you up... or not? Do you think they see you as a *competitor* or a *colleague* in the same network? Really try to see what the intention behind the criticism is.

Part of badassery is being thick-skinned and able to take criticism with a grain of salt because HOW you handle criticism makes all the difference. Also, it is about improving yourself or your work with the criticism that you deem valid and helpful based on the three previously stated criteria. In short, take constructive criticism from those who have walked your path and you are certain that they have your best interest or your customers' best interest at heart. It takes a real badass to be humble and use criticism to up your game.

If I checked myself and my behavior to satisfy every critic that has a problem with an Asian woman being loud, opinionated and willful, I would not have accomplished half the things I did. If I nixed every book idea that didn't get immediate applause from everyone I ran the idea by, I would not be overflowing with creativity and execution for those ideas. If I had played into the perception that a kid from a divorced family who lacked the dominant language skills and income would not prosper and succeed, I would not have reached many of the milestones that I have had in my personal and professional life.

When I was about to publish my first two books, I didn't know the first thing about marketing or *how* to ask friends and fans to support the books' launch short of *"Hey, buy my books!"*. So I followed up with my author mentors in hashing out a game plan. They gave me constructive criticism on how I should approach book bloggers, book festival organizers and fellow authors with bigger fan-bases who were writing in the same genre. One mentor gave me specific feedback on the wording of an email query that I was about to send to people I wanted to solicit to support me on my launch. Another mentor suggested other ways with which I could start building a fanbase, by showing me how he gave back to the writing/publishing community via holding free seminars and serving on speaker panels for other writers.

Before I was about to send the book you are reading off to my editor, I engaged a number of beta readers to go through some chapters and asked for their feedback on the clarity, flow, and organization of the content. You'd better believe I was mentally prepared for all kinds of feedback. If you are a writer and cannot handle criticism, you are in the wrong business. If you deal with showing some kind of craft to other humans, you need to be able to deal with criticism because the constructive kind only helps you become better at what you do – provided you take note. In fact, the only way to avoid criticism is to not do or say anything, and this book and I are definitely NOT about THAT.

What if you decide, at the end of answering my three questions, that a critic is a curmudgeon who just doesn't like anything that you do? What if they haven't done or even attempted what you are doing? What if they have a history of sitting on the sidelines criticizing other people's stuff? What if they don't really understand your audience or customers? Well then, you need to say "Sayonara!" to that critic and their words. You need to put up your thick skin and brush off the criticism and move on. Don't even engage, just move on, because you've got bigger fish to fry and legit criticism to examine in order to do your thing better. I can't recall who said this but when it comes to cynical critics who never have anything constructive to say, *"Their opinions are none of my business."*

3

You are the average of
5 people around you

That's it.

You ARE the AVERAGE of *five* people closest to you.

Let that sink in for a minute. Go ahead. I'll wait.

Since you are the average of five people, what does that make you? Are you high-vibing because the five people with whom you surround yourself are high-vibing? Are you mostly positive and optimistic and can-do because of the company you hang out with? Are you on the track to success or have you already had a series of little victories because your closest friends, colleagues and mentors are also successful? Are you with a tribe who sees the light and walks confidently towards it with a game plan?

Or not? How is that reflected in the company you keep?

Birds of a feather flock together. If you don't want to be a crow, then stop hanging around crows. If you want to soar like an eagle, get to know and fly among eagles.

Listen, I get it. Often we might feel like we cannot escape our social spider web. Maybe the friendships have lasted so long and become so entrenched it feels awkward and even scary not to see people you've been hanging with forever. These could be high school or college friends that you've known for fifteen, twenty, even thirty years. Friends from work, friends in the neighborhood that you run into often, or other parents whose kids have been growing up with your kids; they could be from any of these categories or more.

Remember this though: everything is a choice, including your friendships and the kind of company you keep. It matters little what kind of history you have with someone; for your own personal development and improvement, if you are constantly spending time with negative people, it's only a matter of time and degree that you become negative too. It will become insidious in all areas of your life. If you are hanging around Debbie Downers or Troublesome Teds all the time, guess what that does to your vibe and your own spheres of attraction? Yep, you got it.

It's a matter of deciding what degree of friendship you want to keep with someone, but know that the five people with whom you spend the most time become your sphere of influence. You have to determine if they are lifting you up or if you are the only one doing the lifting. Are they helping you be the best version of yourself or the mediocre version or even a worse version?

Like you, I have hung out with people that are low-vibe. I used to not see it at first but I've become pretty good at seeing their "core" based on the things they tend to say, how they normally behave and the mindsets behind their actions. Now I can spot them a mile away. For your own good and badassery, do stay away from these types of low-vibe people. Let me break it down for you:

- Negative Nancys

  Do you really need someone who has a tendency to rain on your parade all the time? I think not. Why would you need someone who sees the glass half empty nine times out of ten? Think about why and how they are being negative around you. Is it in the language they use to discourage you from doing something you want to do? Is it because they have failed at doing that same thing? Have they not succeeded, so they don't want you to succeed either because they don't want to be left behind? Have they been going through a hard time in their life and that comes out in what they say about *your* goals? Really examine the *why* and *language* of their negativity. Most importantly, move on from them quickly. If they do not want to help themselves out of their perceived doom, it doesn't mean you need to be doomed with them – it means you need to go out and do your thing and prove them wrong. Next!

  I had a coworker at a marketing focus group firm many moons ago who was such a Negative

Nancy; everyone could count on her finding whatever 1-on-1 audience she could after her morning coffee to spout off on whatever ills of her life or of society were happening. It could be gorgeous sunny day and she would say it's too hot and the sun is burning her skin right off when she stepped outside. So yes, many people, yours truly included, avoided running into her in the hallways lest we got caught by the negativity bug.

- Troublesome Teds

They frequently attract shitty trouble like it's going out of style.

Sometimes it's circumstance and sometimes it's just poor fucking choices. Time and again. It's like they need the drama and just can't get the heck out of the hellhole with one shitty drama after another. At some point, you know it's more than circumstance; it's *them*. I don't have the time nor patience to listen to their 20th drama or trouble of the week, and neither do you.

- Gossipy Garys

Good gossip is wonderful and creates bonding among people. If so and so got a well-deserved promotion, so and so is taking a wonderful trip to Italy or some other plum, talk around the water station will be humming. But bad gossip is just spreading bad vibes all around. I mean people talking about a neighbor's or mutual friend's private matters or embarrassing situations; people hatin' on so-and-so's success and talking shit about them with mutual acquaintances and trying to undermine how they became successful; friends doing some backstabbing shit instead of just talking it out with the friends they have a problem with in the first place. Stay away from Gossipy Garys – they are not good for your soul and will drag down your high vibes, big time.

- All-about-me Annas

Notice there are some people who can't stop talking about themselves? When you are trying to share something genuine about yourself, they just somehow revert the focus back to themselves because, oh, the world revolves around them 24/7. You can't cultivate high vibes with people who are all about themselves all the time because their self-absorption does not enable them to see beyond their noses. If they cannot be empathetic listeners, their vibes are low and add nothing to your inner golden circle.

- One-up-you Owens

Ahh yes, the cousin to All-about-me Annas. One-up-you Owens not only hardly listen, whatever you've got, their game is to simply one-up yours. You just had a great vacation in Cancun? They just had an all-expenses comped trip to Europe! You just got promoted? They just wrapped a record year in their own business! You get the point. People who cannot celebrate good news with you for even a moment really cannot be part of your circle – they don't deserve to, either. It goes in the reverse, too. You got into a bad car accident last week and now you are dealing with whiplash? Ha! Two years ago they got T-boned, were laid up in the hospital for two months and needed a steel rod inserted into their hip, followed by six months of physical therapy! The One-up-you Owen's idea of friendship is singular – to one-up whatever you share with them. This kind of person does not vibe high, has no empathy, nor are they a good listener and he doesn't deserve much of your time, if any.

- Jealous Jessies

  Do you know people who just cannot be genu-
  inely happy for someone else because their
  insecurities have their panties twisted up in a
  bunch? If anything good happens to you, they
  have to throw shade by saying some passive-
  aggressive dig – as if you don't truly deserve
  the good thing based on your work or your
  merit. Or, they rain on your parade: Should for-
  tune fall upon your shoulders, they throw cold
  water on them and remind you, "Well, enjoy it
  while you can because it won't last long!" You
  know the type; the jealous streak can come out
  in multiple ways. But in the end, it's all from
  the same root. That person is incapable of being
  part of your high-vibing badassery circle. What
  they need is therapy to work out their issues.
  So cut them loose, sooner rather than later.

- Flaky Freds

  If someone has flaked on you for "last minute
  emergencies" at least three times out of the last
  four times you made plans with each other, it's
  time to reexamine how much energy you want to
  put into that association. Flaky Freds are unreliable and shit seems to happen to them all the time,
  preventing them from keeping appointments or

plans. Sometimes shit does happen but most of the time, Flaky Freds let things happen due to their choices and actions and they are serious commitment-phobes. Again with the choices, people: We each make a series of choices that land us in this exact moment today, this hour, this minute. Flaky Freds are not exempt. They, too, have made a series of choices that rendered them unable to keep promises or plans with others. You also have a choice if you have a Flaky Fred in your circle. You can keep giving them chances and allow excuses for why shit keeps happening so they flake out on plans. Or, you can cut the cord, because unreliable people serve no one and get very little done. Let me add that sometimes Fred may offer no excuses, because he just flat out doesn't feel like honoring a plan or commitment anymore! Flaky Freds are low-vibe people. It's best that you command your inner badasssery and NOT waste time developing a connection with these people. Because quite honestly, they haven't made a concerted effort to connect with you; all the flaking out has robbed the connection.

- Venting Vickies

  Almost like Debbie Downers, Venting Vickies are a whole other level of negativity – the vicious level. Every time you meet up they are seriously complaining or venting about something, as if you have VENTING PUNCHBAG or THERAPIST tattooed on your forehead. The VVs love to unleash their latest complaint about some inequity like a swarm of biblical locusts. People should complain justly when something ill happens, and people should be able to share and confide in close friends about whatever shit is happening in their lives. But you see there IS a difference between them and Venting Vickies whose core – whose essence – is to complain all the damn day, all the damn time. Someone is always doing them wrong, or out to get them. They are always in some kind of stress or turmoil. Something unfair or crappy has always just happened to them on their way over. The moment they get private moment with you, they cannot help themselves in unleashing a serious bout of verbal diarrhea on whatever series of injustices that happened to them that week. You know the type. Scootch them over to the exit of your life. Check, please!

All this is nothing new. You know exactly who these types are in your life; you already see their faces in your mind's eye. Do yourself a favor, assume your badassery and cut cords with these people. They do not serve or deserve your time. They, in no way, lend to the high-vibing friendships you deserve.

At the very least, if you cannot cut them out of your life entirely, limit time spent with these characters as much as you can.

I have, many a time, cut these people out of my life because I just didn't feel good during and after interacting with them. So it was like, *"Sayonara! Don't want what you are dishin' out!"* I'd say that to myself in my head, of course, not out loud so they'd hear me. After I cut them out, my vibe went back way high again. And that's where I like to keep it. When my vibration is high – and when your vibration is high – more awesome things happen. The laws of attraction kick in. You have a more positive outlook and forward progression with goals. All in all, happiness and goodness flow more easily when you eliminate the low-vibing peeps out of your life.

I get that some of these people cannot be avoided, especially if they are your parents, your roommate, your brother-in-law who has been mooching off you for the last two years. But you can, and you must, limit your interaction with them if they impact your vibes negatively. You, hopefully, still have your own private space and sanctuary at your residence to retreat to and maintain your peace and high vibes. You can not pick up calls from the low vibin' people. You do not need to engage with, converse with (for long), or argue back and forth with these low-vibing people, whether you live with them or not.

It's a choice how much time you deal with them. My suggestion is no time at all. The choice to be this badass that you are capable of being is yours. I'm guiding you to the trailhead and it's up to you whether you want to walk on the path to high-vibing greatness.

Now that you know who the stay the hell away from, let's discuss who you SHOULD spend time with:

- **Positive people**

    People who can usually see things in a balanced way, with a majority on the upside, sunny side of things – these are gems. Hang onto them. You'll need them when it rains on your parade. They are your cheerleaders. Attitude is a big part of whether you have happiness or not so much. Positive people have the beauty of choosing positivity. Therefore, they are usually happier, sunnier, can-do kind of people. They should be part of your badass tribe.

    Now, I don't mean for you to stick with people are always naively optimistic, never with a Plan B or not ooking at things realistically. That group includes those who think an outrageous plan will work out no matter what. Those people totally bomb when the plan fails. I mean for you to seek out and keep people who are realistically optimistic with an attitude and demeanor that err on the side of positivity. You see the difference, right?

One of the most beautiful people I've met was an acquaintance from work when I was a sales assistant in my early 20's at a conference/event production company in Santa Monica, California. Well into her fifties, Nada had ash blonde hair and a glow about her. She practiced yoga daily, and always had a genuine smile on her face. I'm pretty sure she's one of those people who have perfected the mantra of "Act as if..." (the manifestation power action). It was no accident that she was one of the top sales closers in the office. No wonder coworkers loved talking with her. I'm sure 'Nada' was her Sanskrit name, she was probably born a Susan or Nancy; but no matter – she was 5'3" of walking & talking Positivity.

- **Active people**

What do I mean by active people? In other words, physically & mentally active anti-slugs.

These types are a wonderful influence in your life, believe me. They can mentally engage you in intellectually stimulating conversation and encourage you to do awesome, physical activities. The best conversations I've had are with friends and strangers who can not only see multiple sides of a story or issue, but can put perspectives in such an intelligent, eureka! way that I walk away feeling high as a kite. In terms of physically active people, do you want friends who are couch potatoes (the work-couch-sleep tribe) or do you want to surround yourself with people who are physically active (and probably pretty healthy) who encourage you to go out and try stuff? It's a no brainer, Badass!

One of my tribes – and I have many, just as you also have many spheres of influence – is hikers. I love hiking and I love hikers; few are as generous with their backpack goods and spirit. Hiking is a wonderful physical activity while you take in gorgeous scenery. I have risen to the challenge many times while hiking peaks of various elevations in California and Utah. While the very summit of Kilimanjaro in Tanzania still eludes me (as of the publishing of this book), don't worry, I will make it back to Tanzania in the near future to try that

19,341-feet beauty. One of my hiking friends is a 73-year-old with the health of a 35-year-old; he hikes and bikes long distance regularly like it's nobody's business. He's mentally sharp, humorous and generally very well-liked by everyone in our hiking circle. He serves as a group leader on many of our hikes. How cool is that?!

People who are mentally and physically active tend to also be the next type of awesome badasses.

- **Action takers / Doers**

  Badasses want to accomplish certain things in their lives. Call those things Bucket List Items or Wish List Must-Dos. Badasses have achievable goals and dreams. We go out and incrementally take actions to make them happen. We don't just wish upon a star and say, *"One day... maybe..."* We take actions toward actualizing what we want. If you are serious about being more of a badass and achieving more of your own goals, you need to hang out with people who are already on track to achieving theirs or have already done so. They know their formula inside out so you can pick their brain for how they got to mastery. High vibers vibe together;

action-takers' high vibes WILL rub off on you in an immensely positive way.

The people I tend to hang out with or talk to frequently, online and offline, are those like me – people who are on track to achieving goals, big and small. Often, they have already achieved something or overcome serious challenges. These are not people who play the victim or wish upon the star because they are action takers and I love them for being such. I, too, bring a huge, positive influence onto the people around me because I'm an action taker and I like giving solicited (and even unsolicited!) advice on how people can take actions, too. Every little incremental action triggers another, and another, and another, and you should be, as I am, constantly getting closer to your big goals. Naturally, I attract others who are action takers and dream makers as well. Inversely, I'm like a moth to a flame toward people who are even bigger action takers than I am. I often say, if I can imagine it, I can do it.

Taking actions toward achieving your dreams sometimes means gambling and taking risks. So look around you, in real life and in the online world. Who are the action-taking badasses that you should surround yourself with? Go and hang out in their world. Go and talk to them and make connections.

- **Humorous people**

  Those with a sense of humor – especially the wicked kind – are awesome. Funny people, those who are able to see the lighter side of things, who can make fun of themselves, or who can call out others' bullshit with a side of sarcasm and humor. Yes, we have our periods of struggle – all the more reason to have the humorous people in our lives to help remind us our grin muscles can still be used. Besides, laughter makes everything better and funny folks are simply terrific.

- **People with a specific skill set that you can learn from – or with whom you can trade skills.**

  Part of life is about acquisition of skills to become better. Some you will master, at others you will remain a lifetime apprentice. There will always be people with skills better than you. Don't resent them; glean from them what works and how they became masters at their craft. On the other hand, there will always be people who are not at your level of skill. Bring those people up and help them rise if you know they wish to improve and they have sought your mentorship – teach them a thing or two and help them become better. Teachers are learners and learners become teachers; and the more you learn, the more you can teach.

However, this is not to say you have to learn everything under the sun. To begin with, you should focus on specializing in one or two things. Mine begin with teaching ESL which I have done for 14 years; then it segwayed to free-lance reporting for newspapers and magazines; and that segwayed to book writing. But I've had to take time to learn and master each craft while slowly gleaning the how-to's from other areas in which I am interested. I have gotten pretty good at the craft of nonfiction writing and publishing that I have an e-course on my website to teach newbie authors how to do it following a process and I have also spoken on panels with writers in the audience and on my own social media platform to share what I know. Book writing/ publishing and speaking about confidence, goal setting and publishing are my focus right now and I choose to use other experts' zones of genius (e.g. web design, branding, best seller campaigning, email list building, business planning) to help me present and market my zones of genius. You know you have only certain amount of time and money right now and to help yourself reach that next level, you will need to entail other people's skills to help you showcase YOUR skills. So find those people; they are not hard to find at all. Again, ask, look around, and the Universe provides.

- **Empathetic & Compassionate people**

  I really, really appreciate empathetic people, partly because I'm not very empathetic myself, especially with my loved ones. What's that saying about getting most frustrated with people you love most... or something to that effect? Yet I can be quite empathetic and compassionate with people that I'm not close to who in dire or sad situations.

  Don't ask me why that is... it's a whole psychology/therapy session for another day.

  I do know that love and empathy make the world go around. Add money to the mix so that it supports our backs, and that is how humanity shows itself.

This is why our family donates money or wish-list goods to needy families every Christmas season; this is why I volunteer for various non-profit organizations with missions I care about deeply (check out my website www.roseanney.com under Philanthropist). Sometimes I engage the help of my family in community events that prepare dry-food packages to send to third world-countries so kids there can be fed. This is why I have been a volunteer mentor with an organization that pairs adult mentors with kids whose family members are dealing with cancer. This is also why I participate every year in a local philanthropic program that packs 4,200 new backpacks full of school supplies and hygiene items for disadvantaged first graders whose household income level falls under a certain level.

Empathy and compassion are why we show up with casseroles, condolent embraces, and money when tragedy befalls a neighbor or a complete stranger.

Empathy and compassion are why we send money, packaged food, canned goods and boxed cereal to the local food pantry so homeless and poverty-stricken families don't have to go hungry for at least a day.

Empathy and compassion are why firefighters and police from neighboring boroughs rushed into the towers on 9/11 to help rescue and recovery efforts.

These are extraordinary humane qualities. We even witness these qualities in some animals. Some friends can be compassionate to a fault, so you keep them but make sure they don't get taken advantage of whenever you can help it. To help others rise via letting your Empathy flag fly is a great thing. If you can surround yourself with a few such people in your circle, it will be a blessing for you.

4

You create your own reality

"Whether you think you can or you think you can't, you are right."

— Henry Ford

"You are the star of your own reality show. It's up to you if you want to have a shitty show with poor ratings or a winning show that gets re-up'ed season after season."

— Roseanney Liu

Henry Ford's quote is one of my favorite quotes of all time. And as you see, I've tweaked it to put my own spin on the same idea.

It's quite simple: The world is the way it is yet we all have different perceptions of how things are and how things operate. This is because we each have our own reality. I probably have a slightly different idea of reality than my husband, the closest person to me. You have different ideas of reality, too, from those closest to you. We see through different lenses, different paradigms. We hold different values and beliefs systems because we come from different backgrounds and experiences.

But the Badass – the person you are becoming – believes and knows the world works in their favor and that whatever they wish for and work for usually becomes reality. This belief is the cornerstone holding up the perception, and therefore, the reality.

I believe in certain things not only because I have so much optimism but also because I expect certain things. I simply don't entertain other options. They're not even in my peripheral vision! Other options are not part of my reality until those other things actually happen.

If you want to play the victim card, guess what? You will indeed have a victim vs. victor situation in which you lose because you have chosen the victim role.

If you are a winner and behave as a winner, your situation and outcome will probably be a happy one. Your perception and attitude will have partially carried you there.

If you believe you don't have what it takes to achieve your dream goal, then you won't.

But if you believe you *do* have what it takes and are prepared to do whatever it takes to achieve your goal, that's your reality and you will make it.

What's the point?

You can and should choose your perception and reality carefully. You are whatever you believe you are. One can choose to think that a woman traveling from California to Tanzania by herself to hike a 19,341-foot high mountain might be scared by the fact that she knows little about the country where it's located. But I chose to look at it as an exciting adventure. I believed – and lived that belief – I would make it to each stop safely while enjoying my adventures in a country (on a continent) I had never been to before.

I created my own reality. Now you can create yours. So, create and think on the side of the good and positivity.

Consider this:

Why do some people have agoraphobia – which is anxiety disorder in which they fear and avoid places that might trigger feelings of entrapment, helplessness, embarrassment or panic – when accidents and awful, random things could happen at home, too?

Why do some people assume the worst about others when the former does not get their way?

Why do some people say, *Bad things just keep on happening to me*? Why does this "bad streak" seem to last weeks, months, years?

None of these things are accidental or a soap opera orchestrated by Fates. Fates are Greek mythical goddesses that were believed to determine human destiny. If you completely believe in Fates and that you have no control over your thoughts, actions and what happens in your life, this book is not for you. You would need to put this book down now – maybe give it to someone else so they can benefit from the content – and go back to watching *The Voice.*

The truth is, life is about a series of actions and consequences. What steers our actions are not random, Fate-designed chess moves. Our own thoughts and beliefs steer our actions. Then, the actions reap a certain set of results and consequences.

I've had friends who complain endlessly about their "stupid, sucky" jobs. Yet they do not talk about what they are doing to end their "stupid, sucky" jobs. Whenever I got together with them, woe-is-me was their topic of the day. It was all about their employment misery and how they wished their boss would just get transferred *or worse.* They wished they didn't have to do x-y-and-z. And yes, maybe their jobs *did* suck. But the bigger question was, what were they doing about it? If this was their perception, their reality, and they didn't like it, what were they doing to bring about change in order to quit bitchin'?

I also have friends who cannot stop harping about the flaws of their spouses. Or how their last half-marathon for a charity had crappy organization. Or how their vacation lodgings out of the country were abhorrent.

They made a choice to focus on the bad and the poor. That became their reality. And I think:

But surely s/he has excellent qualities... that's why you married them?!

But it was for a good cause and by golly, you finished the half-marathon, so good for you and the charity!

But you got to travel and see a different country and the pictures looked amazing... tell me about the wonderful things from this journey!

It's true, we all go through shit sometimes – some more than others and perhaps some much longer than others – but we are not playing the comparison game. The only comparison you should ever have is you versus your former self, or you from yesterday. The point is, we never lose our ability to control our thoughts and how we see ourselves in situations. Responsibility for the quality of perception is on each of us. It is up to us how positive or negative that perception is. From this, we create our reality.

While it sucked for me to almost freeze my butt off at 18,300 feet on Kilimanjaro, in tears, cold and with feelings of disappointment overwhelming me at times, my concluding thought was,

Wow, I made it pretty far on a stunning mountain. I made a trans-Atlantic, intercontinental journey by myself that most people do not get to do in their entire lifetime. Now I know how to better prepare myself for the next time I try to summit this mountain. Because, by the power within myself, I will try again.

While it sucks that no literary agent – out of the five I approached, and I will query more – has chosen to pick up my book proposal for the teen graphic novel, my concluding thought is,

It's ok, I still have to build my fan base and following to make it successful. Whether I have a literary agent and a publishing contract or not, I still know how to independently publish. I know how to publish it well if I decide to do that down the line.

While it sucked to have searing teeth pain before and during my vacation spring 2018 that sometimes I couldn't even sleep, my concluding thought was,

I am so fortunate to have great dental insurance and that it covered most of the expensive root canal procedure I ended up needing to take care of my tooth pain. I'm grateful to have this coverage in order to regain dental health and it's not something everyone has.

While it sucked for me to spend half of my childhood in a divorced household during a time when divorce and kids from single-parent families were still stigmatized, my ongoing thought was,

My mom was so strong that she was able to raise me well on her meager salary. She taught me the value of saving and what a work ethic looked like. I learned to rise above and seize opportunities for myself, even though my divorced, immigrant parent didn't speak the language of the new, dominant culture. I'm so grateful for the opportunity to be independent and stronger, sooner, than my cohorts who grew up with two parents who did speak the dominant language and had well-paid employment. That's my silver lining behind the cloud.

There are often two ways or more to look at a situation. How will you control your perception of a situation, and thereby control your feelings and your reality? If you do not change your perception, perhaps you can change the situation that's bringing about the perception.

It's entirely up to you.

5

Stare fear in the eye

"Being aware of your fear is smart. Over-coming it is the mark of a successful person."

— Seth Godin

Fear is an ugly little monster that only gets bigger if you allow it. Not doing the things you want to do feeds Fear. If you are stopping yourself from living out your badassery or whatever your heart and soul desire, this feeds Fear's enormous appetite.

You need to stop feeding the monster. It does you absolutely no good.

The monster keeps you small and makes you regret not having done the things you really wanted to do.

For example, my concern about hiking a twelve-mile trail to a peak at Baden-Powell in Southern California, by myself, was Fear rearing its head and testing me.

That huge dose of worry and fast heart palpitations when my knee was freshly scraped by coral and bleeding into the Bora Bora ocean where black-tipped sharks were swimming nearby was Fear taunting me.

That two-second eye contact followed by two large, menacing dogs barking at me from across a narrow valley in Hollywood Hills had Fear in overdrive. It took the dogs no time to traverse the bushy hill and chase after me. Fear was in fifth gear, telling me, "I told you so!"

But I would do all those things again. Of course, I'd try harder not to get scraped by coral in any body of water next time. But shit happens sometimes, despite the best preparations.

Life is full of experimentation. Living out loud is doing the things you want to do while trying to be your best self. But you can't truly live life if you allow Fear to set in and take over the driver's seat to control your actions. You can't let Fear hold you back from taking action, either. Do you allow Fear to take control so you overthink about all kinds of things that can go wrong? Does that prevent you from going out and doing things that have the slightest risks? That is no longer life, my friend. That is called being a prisoner.

This is what I do when Fear tries to finagle itself into my driver's seat:

- I think about the likelihood of the worse case scenario happening – the situation that might make me think twice about doing the thing I want to do, such as skydiving when I was twenty-three; or flying to Tanzania by myself at age thirty-nine and hiking Kilimanjaro for six days; or having an onslaught of horrible reviews or zero sales for any of my books.

- If the likelihood of a bad result is minimal for a particular event and I really want to do it, I tell Fear to shut the front door. I move right ahead with planning for the event.

- The planning process gets me all excited and I think about all the wonderful things that could happen as a result of doing that thing. AND I FOCUS ON THE WONDER-FUL POSSIBILITIES as my actions move me toward them.

- I go and aim at having a great time while accomplishing what I set out to do.

That's it, friend. Any over-thinking beyond this four-step process invites Fear back in again. I'm telling you to make no room for that uninvited guest.

It takes practice to stare down Fear, and with some endeavors it might take you many, many attempts before you can overcome Fear's conniving ways. I know that with a better toolkit and a stronger mindset that I can tell Fear to shove it the next time I attempt to summit Kilimanjaro.

Fear was overwhelming and insidious when my group and I set out on the 11:00 PM summiting attempt on October 5, 2017. Several groups of hikers were astir by then, eating biscuits and drinking hot tea provided to us by the porters. I said my blessings internally as the cinnamon taste of the biscuits and the nondescript tea swirled in my mouth. Triple-layering ourselves with synthetic and wool shirts and down jackets, the feeling was somber and my company of hikers hardly spoke with the minor exceptions of checking with one another if we took a dose of the anti-high elevation sickness pill Diamox that night and making sure we got all our water packed and hiking poles ready to go. At this point, my spirit was high despite feeling like I wished I had some protein and more carbohydrates beside the dry biscuits to push my body for the remaining 4,000-feet climb ahead of me. Fear hadn't reared its ugly head yet.

We started our hike up away from base camp Kibo by 11:30 PM and all was quiet. It seemed that we were the second group of people to leave camp, after the large group of German college students. My eyes felt dry and stung within the first 20 minutes from the bitter cold that greeted us from the mountain. *"You think it's that easy to walk through my door and come into my house, don't you,"* the mountain challenged. I tried to ignore it but soon I could not see beyond 20 feet around me in the darkness of midnight. From starting in the middle of the pack in our group of eight, I soon trailed toward the back of the group as I didn't want to hold up anyone. The enormous elevation gain meant I had better hike at a slower pace because rushing it and risk getting acute mountain sickness was not part of my game plan. Darkness started chuckling at me as I put my left hand on the back of my lead guide's shoulder ahead of me and my right hand dug into my hiking pole. I had on ski gloves but in the first hour I felt the searing cold, the cold that's so extreme it felt like fire burning my hand instead. Fear was checking in with me, *"Hello dear. Soon you won't be able to feel your hands at all. So enjoy the hike while you can."*

Shapes and moving objects were discernible within 20 feet around me but beyond that it was just gray snow all around. The upward switchbacks seemed interminable as I put one foot in front of another. *"Pole-pole,"* (pronounced "polay-polay", Swahili meaning "Slowly, slowly") the guides reminded us. Indeed, no one had the energy or the wherewithal to talk or to race up the summit in that cold and with that elevation gain. It felt like every step took three seconds, and energy and core warmth needed to be conserved as much as possible. My eyes were stinging and sending down tears on my semi-frozen face due to the dry cold air as well as my not being able to feel most of the nerves in my hands and feet. "I. CAN. DO. THIS," I chanted to myself for another hour. Maybe longer. Time on the cold mountain during the night hike seemed to stop like it does in Vegas casinos.

"STOP! We have lost touch with most nerves!" my hands and feet screamed at me.

"It's just Fear trying to trick you,"I told them. I took many 20-second breaks, with my guide next to me, to drink the warm tea and to take my hands out of my measly ski gloves that barely protected me and put my hands against the skin of my stomach to try and regain some warmth and feeling.

"Come on, Ro. We can't stay put for long. It invites core temperature to drop when we stay here too long," my guide encouraged me to put my gloves back on and move on.

I willed my feet to trudge on and for my right gloved hand to wrap itself around the handle of my pole and it barely did. It was hard to control my hands once their nerves were no longer on speaking terms with my brain as Cold and Fear were throwing a party together against me and my fellow hikers.

Somewhere around 17,000 feet the younger of the Norwegian sisters in our group supposedly got really sick – acute mountain sickness with vomiting and headaches. I say supposedly because I didn't see her most of the way as I was in the back of the group and I was in my head wrestling with my own demons. You couldn't wait out the symptoms at that altitude and in that cold. Later she told me she was saying to her older sister that she felt sick and really bad and her sister kept telling her to tough it out. The younger sister made a decision to descend the mountain and one of the taller porters – a sort of soldier like the character, Mountain, from *Game of Thrones* – carried her down. Speedy descent was key and she was quite sick. I felt bad for her and I was still fighting my battle against Fear and Cold, thinking I had a chance, so I moved on, slowly but surely with my guide just a couple of feet ahead of me.

My eyes wouldn't stop producing tears, trying to protect me however little they could against the stabbing freezing air. The tears almost immediately crystallized as they streamed down my face. I lost count of how many times I took my gloves off to breathe some semblance of warmth and life back into my hands, to no avail. The mountain and its climate made the most unkind host at night, sending its agent Fear to break me down limb by limb, starting with my fingers. I finally felt the formidableness of my opponent whom I had embraced during the day and even the previous nights when we were not trekking; but now, the mountain was chewing me up and I wondered how long before I could reach the summit, before it would spit me out with frostbitten limbs.

"How much longer? " I asked my guide at what felt like every 30-minute interval.

"Not too long, Ro. At this pace, maybe another two hours," he said.

Two hours in "normal" southern California climate condition in October is beautiful and doable for a hike, even against high elevation. But this was Kilimanjaro and this was the dead of night; this mountain makes its micro-climates that seemed to have their own plans for hikers.

I became slower in my steps. "I......CAN..... DO.....IT....." was each word corresponding with each step forward and up in what seemed to take 3-4 seconds per word/step. I couldn't wrap my head around the supposed two more hours of this.

"You think you can come here with your California ski gloves that did their job in Colorado in the winter and that you'd summit Kili on your first attempt? You are quite naïve, aren't you, lady?" Fear taunted.

And around 18,000 feet I was breaking down; I took even more breaks to wipe away tears and to will feeling back into my stubborn frozen, stiff hands. Using my core skin and accepting my guide's encouragement to put my hands against the skin of his lats too when my own skin was no longer doing a damn thing, my hands were dying and whispering, *"Warm us now or we die."* Now I was visibly upset and shaking. Have I traveled 9,776 miles to a different continent to not achieve what I set out to do? To not achieve the goal I trained for 6 months to do?

Fear laughed, *"You could summit, maybe, but you will lose your hands, permanently."*

I cried some more as I put one boot in front the other, dragging my feet a bit in the narrow snow patchy path. I could hardly see my own bootprints and wondered if I had imagined that moonlight that showed them earlier. I was starting to believe Fear, which can sound convincing when you are not of sound mind and body. "I….CAN…DO…THIS…" started to juxtapose with "I….HATE…THIS.." I could not wrap my head around losing my hands and maybe feet to frostbite in order to trek another 1,300+ feet when summit and sunrise would finally greet me. Fear was getting to me, big time.

My guide took breaks next to me, both coddling me for the breaks and being the authoritative parent telling me I needed to move on when my sit-down time had expired. "We can descend any time you want, Ro," he said. "But we are just under Gilman's Point now. Maybe another hour we will reach that point and another hour for the Uhuru peak [the summit]."

"Ok," I replied. *No, we can't!* my hands screamed, their voices getting fainter but still sharp enough for me to hear as they were drowning in an abyss of numbness. *We have to descend NOW, or we will never type or write again! We will never wrap ourselves around a hot mug of coffee again or feel the soft, little faces of your kids!*

Fear's tears opened the flood gates wide by now, even my nose was sniffling. Sadness, disappointment, shock at the idea of not achieving what I thought was an achievable goal, and fear were all rolled up and exiting my body via my tears.

At around 18,300 feet, just below Gilman's Point, I made the decision to descend. A mere 1,141 feet away from my goal, I chose to believe Fear and save my frozen hands from what could have gone on to be irreversible frostbite. The African sunrise said *Jumbo!* to me as my guide and I descended quickly together, and regret as well as awe for the jagged Mawenzi peak before me burst into my heart. We stopped a few times to admire the beauty of the Tanzanian mountainscape and the views beneath, the sunrise more paternal and encouraging than the night air and the ascent.

"You can come back anytime, dear, and try again," the sun and Mawenzi offered me.

Fear and I had a face-off on Kilimanjaro and it won, that time, and left me with the worst feeling in the world: regret. I had underestimated and under-prepared for this enormous trek and its own climate. But I did look at Fear in its eye and made a decision to spare my hands that cold early morning in October. The mountain will always be there and I'll be more prepared to attempt summiting again.

The key to remember, friend, is that it's more than okay to face your fear, to come to grips with what Fear is saying vs what you are really saying yourself. It's more than okay to try something again despite it not working out in your favor the first time – or the first 100 times. Fear wants you to forfeit and stay home, but every time you and I show up, we are not giving up, and every time we make the attempt again, we get closer to beating Fear at its own game as we are smarter, faster, and better with each attempt. So please – do whatever you can to learn, to prepare and to stare down Fear; in doing so do we find the courage live out loud and achieve our goals.

6

Contentedness breeds laziness & lack of imagination; do more than just coast

"The difference between successful and unsuccessful people is that the successful ones are willing to do the things unsuccessful people are not willing to do."

— Jeff Olson

"I do not think there is any thrill that can go through the human heart like that felt by the inventor as he sees some creation of the brain unfolding to success... such emotions make a man forget food, sleep, friends, love, everything."

— Nikola Tesla

Life is about learning and living. If you aren't learning and applying something new, frequently, you are doing life wrong. You are most certainly doing Badassery 101 wrong. Although we are sometimes teachers, we are always lifelong students. So pick the things you want to learn or become much better at; find your mentors and role models, and by all means, learn from them and practically apply what you learn for your situation. For my writing business, I constantly learn from authorpreneurs who have come before me in such aspects as how to build a readership, how to write productively, how to structure a nonfiction book in such a way that it reads more clearly and usefully for the audience, how to utilize various marketing channels available to authors, etc. For my speaking business, I learn from my role models on how to pitch correctly to event organizers, how to be their allies in custom-tailoring my talks so that their audiences get maximum benefit. My role models also show me nitty gritty stuff like how to find events at which I can speak, how far in advance to pitch, and the things that come into play when negotiating my speaking fee. I am constantly learning in both industries, and the learning makes my brain frustrated yet happy at the same time. This is what I want for you as you assume Badassery: learn whatever it is you want to learn; create whatever it is you want to create. First, you will be an apprentice. Over time you will master things and be able to teach those that come after you. A teacher is simply someone who knows a few things more than you, and has the clarity and patience to teach. Eventually, you will reach master level in the skill you learn to acquire.

This learning process is pure Badassery; it is pushing against your own learning curve and intellectual limits. It is expanding your horizon beyond the status quo, beyond what you already know. I want you to venture into unknown territory to learn how to do something better. This is part of Badassery 101.

Sometimes it has nothing to do with business. If you want to learn a certain craft or skill for leisure, so many avenues are available to guide you on your learning path. Not the least of these avenues are YouTube, Udemy, Teachable, local instructors, and people you know in your circles. Have you always wanted to learn how to play the guitar? Spend the time and money and take lessons. Have you always wanted to know how to skateboard or surf? Spend the time and money, and take lessons. Or, teach yourself by watching a lot of videos. That's why YouTube and Udemy are a godsend. Waste not these great learning platforms.

Make the time and save the money towards acquiring the skill you want to have. Life is about doing life a little better than how we did it yesterday, or the day before or last month. Pick something you are highly keen on learning and by all means, learn it. Pick two or more if you like. Learning how to do something can be frustrating, yet it's a sure-fire way to boost your badass confidence. When you learn, incrementally, how to do something that's difficult at first for you, confidence peaks out of the soil. When you can see evidence of growth, and you start learning to ask the right questions and apply your learning the right way, confidence flowers. When you become so good at something that people tell you that your stuff is good - and you believe it – your badassery skyrockets.

Please do give yourself the opportunity to learn and grow at something.

Here's a bit of a tangent:

How many people do you know that let life get in the way so they leave by the wayside something they really wanted to pursue? It might be a goal, a skill, a hobby, an invention, anything they wanted to do better. But they don't do it and just live their lives predictably, every day, by the status quo? They are like Homer – the one from *The Simpsons*, not *The Iliad* – content to do the bare minimum at an hourly wage job. They come home, pop a beer and sit in front of the TV for the whole night. Rinse and repeat the next day.

Are you like Homer too?

Do you know how boring that is, and what a big disservice that is to your life as a human being?

News flash: IT IS!

You picked up this book because you wanted to be better, some way, some how. There's not a more sure-fire way to improve yourself than to apply the tenets being shouted at you from this chapter. *Hello, can you hear me now??!!*

Find the thing(s) you want to improve, or a skill you want to acquire. Search out all methods that your finances and time allow you to apply. If you don't have enough money or time to apply to that skill, find ways to make more money and time. And do them!

Too many parents are guilty of this: It's like they suddenly become hobby-free and passion-free once a child comes into the picture. Then, it's all about the baby and developing the kid's unknown talents. Or worse, it becomes all about pouring an ungodly amount of money and time and chauffeuring to develop that kid's talents in a zillion different activities. At the same time. Before the kid turns twelve.

Please don't stop focusing on improving yourself and pursuing your own goals and hobbies and inventive ideas – whether or not you are raising kids. In fact, one of the best ways to role-model for your children is to show them that you consistently pursue things that are important to YOU and have nothing to do with your J-O-B. Show them that you still practice electric guitar and throw in jam sessions with your old (or new!) bandmates. Show them that mindfulness practice, or yoga, or whatever method helps you relax and become centered is important to you. Invite them to share your practice and techniques as it would benefit them too. Show them the latest thing that you are working on for your side project and, if they are old enough, solicit their feedback. Ask them if they'd like to help you with a specific part of this project.

My kids are ages eleven and eight of the publishing date of this book. I try to involve them in two of the things I do: hiking and the creative part of book writing.

If I know a hike I have planned is relatively short, six miles or less, and the route is scenic and it's not a far drive, I usually invite my family to come on the hike with me. We all join the group I'm signed up with. Sometimes they moan and complain before and during the hike, but we – yes, all of us – end up having the best time by seeing new sights on foot, seeing the scenery at a new elevation, and chatting with other hikers.

When I'm in the creative part of the writing process such as reviewing or considering cover design concepts, or looking at collateral for the book launch, I share those with my family. I solicit their input and ask them to share why they think they do about the book covers or the title and what-have-you. They know writing is a big part of who I am and a vehicle to make one of my life missions happen. They enjoy seeing and participating in the creative process.

So the bottom line is, live your best life by pursuing the goals you want for yourself. Don't forget them or forsake them just because you are busy raising kids or making money for other people's businesses. Kids are going to leave the nest one day and you probably have zero to little equity in someone else's business, so you should not put your own goals on hold for umpteen years.

I wasn't born a writer or a teacher or a speaker or a hiker. I've had to learn how to *be* those roles and partake of the activities entailed therein. I'm still learning everytime I am assuming one of those roles, and I love it! The learning curve is steep in certain things sometimes, but I love the learning process. and I want to be better at those specific things – I owe it to myself and to my life to learn and apply what I want to do. That is the very essence of being at the apex of the animal kingdom. Humans are not just here on Earth for survival; one of the reasons we are "better" than other animals in the hierarchy is because we are constantly learning how to do things better. We owe it to ourselves and our civilization to make everything we do – and what we come in contact with – better than the generation that came before ours. To do that, first we need to improve ourselves by living out the process of skills acquisition. From that process, we might realize an idea or an invention that will make everything even better! The eureka! of cool concepts and inventions sometimes come out of necessity, not just imagination. You will know what should come out of necessity only when you apply the learning process yourself.

When I was about to publish my first two books, I thought a project management worksheet or online tool would come in handy. I was managing all of the pieces of one publishing project and answering questions for the project manager of the other book, simultaneously. I was dealing with questions - some of which I didn't even know I should have asked until issues came up - with my subcontractors; the editors, the cover designer, the formatter, the distributor, and the printer. Questions spanned from costs to turnaround time, to nuances that pertained to only certain subcontractors such as gutter width, page bleed, font, table of contents layout and more. During several months of back-and-forth period with several subcontractors, I wished that I had a project management tool that would enable me to see, ahead of time, when each piece should happen, what piece would follow what other piece, and what questions I needed to get ready for dealing with a particular issue.

Out of this *"I wish I had"* situation, I developed my own project management sheet which is a bonus item I provide to students in my how-to-self-publish course, which is available on my website under the Store tab.

Out of necessity and a wish list came an inventive tool that I developed for those that come after me in the self-publishing process. It happened because I was in the middle of acquiring a skill – the skill of self-publishing a book from scratch.

An inventive idea will happen because sometimes you are purely curious. A curious mind is an awful thing to waste. If Nicola Tesla hadn't been a curious young man, it might have taken society much longer to obtain alternating current electrical power. Later, it became the basis for the long distance power behind Westinghouse, the hydroelectric power plant, and the coil for wireless and radio technologies. All that came about because Tesla was such a curious boy.

So please don't be content. Be a badass and learn some new things for the pure pleasure of learning or to improve upon some existent thing(s). Just when you think you are doing pretty good, take a breath and congratulate yourself but the next day you have to start planning on how you can do better, how to outdo your former self. You will be frustrated, yet wonderfully happy, growing your capacity for learning.

7

Tell Perfection to take a hike and just do it.

If I waited for perfection, I would never write a word.

— Margaret Atwood

Few brands are as recognizable and universally understandable as Nike's *"Just do it."* and for great reasons. And many have uttered a similar message as Margaret Atwood's in her quote above.

The same are applicable to one's Badassery.

You as the badass need to **not wait** for Perfection. Don't wait for the following:

- A number of tried and true methods
- Validation from other people
- When you no longer feel Fear

You are never going to feel completely ready, and not enough of those things are ever going to happen to *make* you ready. The chasing of Perfection is overrated and literally slows down actual production and action of the thing you want to do.

Truth: Your first shot out of the gate at what you want to do is NEVER going to be PERFECT. That is why it's important to prepare the best you can, then pull the trigger and run out the gate to do that thing. But the more attempts you make, the closer to Excellent you become. So if you have to chase something, chase Excellence, as Perfection is a mirage that does not actually exist.

Examples:

I gave myself a year to research on how to self-publish. I prepped by attending as many webinars and seminars as I could. I read books on the topic, gleaning as much as I could. I networked and went to events for authors. Towards the end of that year, I started writing my heart out.

Did I feel completely ready to publish my own books at the end of that year? Not quite.

Did I do it anyway and did I learn a ton along the way? Yes! In fact, I got my first two books published at the same time and wow, the learning curve was steep. I learned so much about what I didn't even know to ask.

As the youngest pledge member of the coed business fraternity on campus eons ago, I ran for the position of Chancellor of the chapter shortly after I completed my pledging period. The doubt of *Why would the more senior members of the chapter vote for me, a Freshman, when I don't have the slightest clue how to be huge figurehead at fraternity meetings and ceremonies?* crossed my mind for a second.

But, there was no better way to prepare myself for the position other than (a) interviewing former Chancellors of my chapter; (2) amassing all the confidence I could muster to run for election with a kick-ass speech; and (3) getting elected and doing my very best upholding the St. Roberts' rules of presiding over chapter meetings and ceremonies.

Well, (1) and (2) got me elected and I did the best I could with (3) during the semester that I served as Chancellor, so much so that several members told me I should have run again for that position for the following semester. Now have I made mistakes while serving in that position? Yes! But I learned from those mistakes and tried not to repeat them as I continued serving in that role.

I gave myself six months to train to hike Mount Kilimanjaro in spring/summer 2017.

Would most people say, *"That's long enough"*? Or would they say that was not the "perfect" amount of time to train for the feat? Maybe, maybe not. Who cares? Other people's standards and opinions are none of my business.

Were the hike conditions and my summiting attempt perfect? Not by a long shot, especially on the second to last day and on summiting night at 11:30 PM. But, I had prepared the best I could and gave myself a timeline to train and a deadline. I pulled the trigger to hike Kili during one of the best months for the most popular route with a 90+% summiting success rate. I learned so much from that six-day journey and that mountain, and I know I'm smarter for it and can probably do it better during my second attempt. Now, will the second attempt be perfect? Who knows? Maybe, maybe not. But nothing will keep me from trying again, least of all Perfection, because as I said, it's overrated. I will not let the idea of having perfect conditions stop me from doing what I want to do.

And neither should you.

In fact, I have said to people, "Fail fast and fail hard." I have heard other people say this too. Sometimes it is in the failure that we learn about who we are and how to do something much better in subsequent attempts. Mastery comes out of having failed at something, not from doing it perfectly the first time. It can take multiple times... think of Edison's and Tesla's experiments.

Tell Perfection to take a hike. Do your best in the research, the prep work and talking to everyone under the sun about your next project idea, but by all means, set a deadline to pull the trigger on launching this new venture or project. It's not going to be perfect but you WILL learn how to make it better and better along the way. First, you have to take that first step towards the "way."

8

Always trust your feelings and instincts but beware of "irrational" fears

One of the tenets of Badassery 101 is that badasses follow their instincts and pursue their desires no matter what anyone else says.

How many times did people talk you out of doing something you really wanted because their logic or *their* fear made sense at the time, and then you regretted not following your heart?

How many times did you say to yourself, *"Oh man, I should have done this!"* or *"If only I had trusted myself* and _____ wouldn't have happened"?

Badasses trust their instincts and gut feelings. Non-badasses get talked into shit.

There. It's as simple as that.

Now, take note: I'm not saying don't do your research or don't examine all the pros and cons before making a big decision. In fact, you should do all of that.

Just know that sometimes – often, actually – your instincts, your gut feelings are very powerful. They are trying to steer you in the right direction that either keeps you safe or makes you happy.

Many times, on unmarked hiking trails, I have trusted my instincts. *This direction doesn't feel right anymore. This area doesn't seem well-trekked at all.* So I stopped and redirected myself. Or I checked my trails app to get on the right path again.

There have also been times when I felt rushed into business contracts that I was excited about and I chose to ignore the little voice – *Instinct!* – in the back of my head. It was saying I should wait and conduct more due diligence to check out the other parties first no matter how great the contract or the people on the other side of the deal seemed. I had to suffer in lost time and money when the other parties didn't hold up their end of the bargain. *Now if only I had listened to that tiny voice Instinct, that was trying to keep me safe.* For example, in 2011, I thought I wanted to be a party planner for people with big budgets in a particular area of Los Angeles. I had no experience, no contacts, just a whim that I would like to help people throw fabulous parties and get paid. I responded to an ad on Craigslist from a children's party planner who was seeking a business partner. I met the woman behind the ad on a Friday, had lunch and dinner with her to get to know her and the business, and before you know it, I was handing her a check for a lot of money for a business partnership. I let my excitement overwhelm my instinct because I didn't want to offend her with "*I'll think about it*" and maybe lose my opportunity. Instinct was trying to tell me "*Slow your roll, Ro! Check her past client references! Check her BBB standing! Check her inventory.*" I did none of that. I was feeling a lot of a regret a couple of days later, realizing that I wasn't ready to be a partner in a children's party planning business. I called and emailed her, asking her to honor the three-day rescission period in our contract, which stipulated my right to get my money back.

Was she professional and did she honor the rescission period? You guessed it. Nope! I spent months dragging it out in Small Claims court trying to get my money back. It involved trying to track her down – very hard when the woman turned out to be a con artist – paying an additional $600 in fees for a business attorney to represent me in correspondence and in court once when the other party finally showed her face, and filing a bunch of paperwork for the claim. Although I ultimately won, it was to no avail. It's impossible to get someone to pay you money owed when they cannot be found and served papers by the sheriff.

I learned my lesson – to trust my instinct.

Trust your badass instinct, friend. It only exists to serve you and usually works in conjunction with common sense. Sometimes things get in the way; other people, social norms, past history. They try to obstruct you from fully feeling and following your instinct. That is when you need to quiet the other voices and let Instinct speak more loudly on its own in your mind and trust it. I was "afraid" of offending that woman and "afraid" of losing an opportunity. Fear totally told my instinct to shut up. That was my mistake in letting Fear take over instead of letting Instinct have the floor.

Do understand, however, your instinct sounds different from irrational fears. Your instinct may be telling you to not get on that plane for a flight to Texas because you can smell alcohol on the pilot passing by. This is different from fearing the plane will crash every time you take a flight. Your instinct not to drive further into a sketchy neighborhood is not wrong when your cell reception is next to nil and the people on the sidewalks are looking at you kind of funny. This is different from believing you will get robbed and left for dead by traveling to a new country – so you don't travel at all. Your instinct to not buy into a seemingly wealthy, jet-setting entrepreneur's program that sounds awesome when his customer service team sucks at answering questions is different from your irrational fear that *all* online programs are out to scam people. Just because you heard your neighbor or cousin got scammed by a couple of online entrepreneurs doesn't mean you will too.

We have to quiet our minds sometimes to really hear the voices of Instinct and Rationale. Don't let yourself be ruled by irrational fears that have no basis in history, science or probability.

How many people – especially women - do you know have unintentionally shut down their instinct because societal norms that raised them to be "nice" told them to smile and accept whatever impropriety or rudeness that came their way? How many times have you not spoken up for yourself or not done the right thing because the ways in which you were conditioned taught you to behave a certain way that's opposite of how Instinct was trying to save you? Next time, whatever shit that's about to go down, just trust your instinct – it only exists to protect you.

9

Stand up for yourself and for others

"Be sure you put your feet in the right place, then stand firm."

— Abraham Lincoln

"Let's continue to stand up for those who are vulnerable to being left out or marginalized."

— Hillary Clinton

Whether in the moment or over a long period of time, few things are as badass as standing up for yourself and for others whose voice may not be as strong as yours. Exercising your voice and standing up for what you believe is right takes action and energy. To do so against what seems to be a majority against your position takes bravery. Not everyone is brave. To exercise your action, energy and bravery in one shot, over and over again, takes a real badass. I cannot encourage you enough to do that and thereby contribute your part in making your life better and our world a better place.

Speaking up and standing up for yourself means advocating for your rights and standing firm by what you are willing to accept. It also means walking away from what you will not tolerate and fighting against what isn't right. How many times have you heard that friend who continues to put herself in jeopardy, and maybe her children, too, because of an abusive domestic partner? How many times have you allowed your boss talk down to you a certain way that completely annihilates your self worth? How many times have you simply let one person and their five friends cut in front you in line when you have been waiting forty-five minutes already and each additional person ahead of you adds another five-minute wait?

Once or twice?

Never? Good for you.

But how about this:

When you are the passenger in your black friend's car, how much are you going to push back against the cop that pulls you both over the side of the road for no reason? How about if s/he demands to see your friend's license and registration and calls in his license to the dispatch without telling you why they pulled your friend's car over while neither you nor your friend has the slightest clue what he did wrong? Maybe it's that you guys are just in the wrong place at the wrong time and he's supposedly the wrong skin color to this cop?

How much are you going to stand up for you friend and question the cop about why the heck you guys are being pulled over? Because you know as well as I do, this situation happens ALL THE TIME in this America.

Or how about when a VIP frequent flyer male passenger in his 50s is sexually harassing a fellow passenger in business cabin, and the cabin crew does not say anything to stop the male passenger? In fact, they keep on serving him alcoholic beverages, giving him more audacity to behave in a blatantly inappropriate and illegal way on an airplane because, oh, he's a VIP frequent flyer. You can see everything as it happens because you are just one row over.

Would you stand up and say something for the female passenger being harassed? Would you videotape the incident unfolding with nary a flight attendant or captain doing anything to stop it? Would you tell them that they'd better stop serving the man, pull him aside and tell him to stop acting like a fool, otherwise the airline is going to have a shit-storm of a PR nightmare on their hands because you are going to put your three thousand-plus Twitter followers to good use?

How about when the American establishment does the most un-American thing in June 2018 by literally tearing children who are minors – some as young as babies and toddlers – away from their parents at the

U.S.-Mexico border – in order to punish and deter further illegal immigration while leaving those children in triple-digit degreed encampment for who knows how long. Are you going to donate money towards the cause against this travesty or are you going to call your state's senators and house of reps that tell them this Hitler-esque atrocity will NOT stand and they'd better stop this or else they can kiss their re-election goodbye? Or are you going to stand by and do nothing because they "aren't your children"?

I hate to sound like your mother but here it goes:

You are not here to be Mr. or Ms. Popular or Miss Don't-Make-Waves. You are here to live your best life while doing the right thing. The right thing is sometimes hard to do. Sometimes it's not even clear right away what the right thing is, but the right thing is always right and it always emerges. Too many side effects happen when you don't speak up for yourself or for others around you when they are being wronged. These side effects are not limited to:

- Regret
- Not sleeping well
- A *verklempt*, closed feeling in your chest
- Sadness
- Proliferation of social injustice

Please don't take part in these ills of your life and of society.

Do speak your truth, do stand up for yourself when you feel your rights are being infringed upon, and do the same for others when others are being trespassed upon.

Here's the thing: There will always be fools and baddies trying to take advantage of you. There will always be someone trying to hurt you and others. They are operating Evil 5.0 and their viruses are downright nasty. If you don't debug and do something to fight against their viruses the moment you see or experience them, they will only grow like cancer and suffocate you and those around you. Stiffen up your spine and put a stop to the cancer they spread by using whatever means and tools available to you. The one tool we all have in common is our voice. When you see something wrong, say something out loud against it. Let the perpetrator know you see it, you are watching them, and what they do is unacceptable and will not be tolerated. This is badassery and always the right thing to do.

In April, 2018, I was so happy to see, via video, at least two white bystanders not bystanding at all inside the Starbucks in Philadelphia. They were videotaped telling the cops that the two black men they were arresting did nothing wrong at all even though they didn't order anything from the menu. They were just there waiting for someone. Inside a Starbucks! Apparently if you are black and waiting for someone, you cannot do it inside a Starbucks lest an employee call 9-1-1 on you.

Starbucks issued a public apology to the black men and said in a statement to *Good Morning America*:

> "The circumstances surrounding the incident and the outcome in our store on Thursday were reprehensible, they were wrong," Starbucks CEO Kevin Johnson said. "And for that, I personally apologize to the two gentlemen who visited our store."
>
> Johnson added this scenario was "completely inappropriate to engage the police." He said that Starbucks would be providing more training for its store managers, particularly training against unconscious bias.
>
> (from Time.com, April 16, 2018)

But would the apology have happened if there were no video footage of the stupid arrest? Would it have happened if the bystanders standing up for the black men were not white?

Sometimes it takes a social media shit-storm, and a crowd, to right a wrong. But that is what we have come to in our society. Unfortunate, but true.

If there are fences, please be on the right side of the fence and speak up for what's right even when you are not personally or directly affected, even when your skin color or socioeconomic background isn't the same as the victims. Speak up even when no media is involved, when no cameras are rolling, when it may not directly affect how well you sleep that night.

That was a true story in February 2018 about the VIP passenger on a major airline sexually harassing another passenger. There had already been tens of thousands of outraged comments and support for the woman following the woman's public report to the airline. She had posted on social media about the three hours of harassment hell she experienced. I did not need to pile on the comments as that would have added no value. Instead, I in-mailed via LinkedIn the VP of Airport Operations & Customer Service and asked him what the company would do about this male passenger who was harassing the woman. I told him my sentiment that not only was his behavior downright unacceptable but that the flight crew's tolerance of his behavior was equally unacceptable. Within hours, he wrote back,

"Roseanney, what our guest shared via Facebook is very disturbing. We have launched an investigation and have revoked this passenger's travel privileges pending the outcome of that investigation. A number of executives have spoken with her this evening. She is actively engaged in helping us with both the internal and external investigation related to this incident. Take care. /J."

Two weeks passed and I heard nothing on social media of what the airline had done. I in-mailed the same executive again to follow up. He responded,

"Roseanney, my apologies for the delayed response. I've been out of the country for the last week. Trust we're committed to doing our part to address the issue of sexual misconduct on our flights. We've begun work with our employees and union leadership to design a training program that will begin in early 2018 to address this topic – designing with perspectives from guests, crews, labor and other partners. Our goal is to create an environment where guests and employees alike feel protected and empowered, and where customers have a safe and enjoyable

travel experience. At this point, the individ-
ual in question is still banned from traveling
*on ******** Airlines. Take care." /.J.*

Yes! Banned from the airline! I hope he gets banned from every airline. The fool can walk from A to B to get to places if he cannot keep his lewd comments about other passengers to himself. That is the very least an entity in power can do, and that came from a collective of thousands of voices that stood up with the woman against the atrocities she endured during that flight. The result of this incident shows what happens when society works collectively in the right direction.

I want you, and me, and all of us to always strive to be part of that right direction, by speaking up and standing up for ourselves and for others when their voice isn't as loud or as strong. Together, we ARE strong and we CAN do the right thing. This, is what badasses do.

10

Get out of your well

One day, Toad came upon a well and looked in.

"Hello there?! Anyone down there?!" the curious Toad hollered down.

"Oh hi! How are you?" Frog answered from deep on the bottom of the well.

"I'm good. How are you? What are you doing down there?"

"Well, I live here," answered Frog.

"Down there in the well? By yourself? Well, it's such a nice day out... why don't you come up and join me on a stroll to the lily pads?" Toad invited merrily.

"No, thanks, I'm good. I can see the patch of sky from here, I know it's a nice day out."

"But, don't you want to hop on the lily pads?" Toad cajoled.

"Nah, it's ok. I got paintings of lily pads right on my wall down here," Frog replied.

"But those are paintings. I mean *real* lily pads. What about that cool new bridge Otter and his family built? Let's go check that out," Toad tried again.

"Oh I don't need to see any bridges. I got a cool old rope down here I can swing on any time I feel like it."

"But that's just a dirty old rope you've seen forever. What about visiting beloved Deer and her new doe? I heard she's a beauty. Come on, let's go visit Deer and family in the forest…it's a nice a day for a walk."

"No, I'm good. Tell Deer I said 'Congratulations', alright? I'm just going to lay out here on my little patio chair, look up at the patch of sky and enjoy some light reading."

"Is there anything I can do to help you come out of the well to enjoy what's out here? Even for just a few hours?" Toad tried one last time.

"Probably not. I'm good, really. Have a great day ok?" Frog replied.

****

This is the gist of an old story that was told to me when I was a little kid in Taiwan. My classmates and I at the time had various silly answers when the teacher asked us if we were Frog, what could get us out of the well. Answers ranged from seeing Deer's new baby, to finding candy in the forest, to going swimming in the lake and a whole host of other options the story didn't even supply. But I doubt those would have moved Frog. He was stuck in his own well.

While I also believe *to each their own*, and we all do like different things, what puzzles me is how people could not like traveling. Despite the minor annoyances, don't the benefits to traveling far outweigh the negatives?

To state the obvious, traveling increases your badassery and your confidence mojo because it:

- Pushes beyond fear and limitations set by your comfort zone – since you are physically in a different place that you are not familiar with. Fears are multiplied when one travels to other countries where language and customs are different from their native countries, but by doing it anyway, your mind feels a boost of confidence that you've got this, you *can* do this.

- Your mind and skill set have no choice but to expand. In seeing new ways of doing things and experiencing different systems such as language, transportation, customer service, lines, how people converse, how people treat their surroundings and each other. your mental horizon expands beyond what you are used to. Your skills are challenged and exercised by having to communicate your needs and wants, by having to navigate, by having to observe and demonstrate acceptable behavior. You have no choice but to start adapting because you have to quickly get from survival mode to a thriving and productive mode. This growth is badassery in and of itself. Traveling is the quickest, surefire way to deliver this type of growth.

- By traveling, your senses are exposed to many different things. Some of these things will inspire you to do and see things differently – and perhaps more positively – once you get back to home base.

There's a saying by a wise person:

The most comfortable person is one who has been in many uncomfortable places already.

And,

Be willing to be uncomfortable. Be comfortable being uncomfortable. It may bet tough, but it's a small price to pay for living a dream.

— Peter McWilliams

No situation can deliver a more discomforting feeling than traveling – especially by yourself – to other countries where the language, culture and customs are different. You'll be uncomfortable a lot at first because you are no longer dominant or even good in anything in that new place. You are a visitor, subject to the new land's rules which you are still learning. If you do the wrong thing or say the wrong thing you can offend someone. If you go the wrong way, you can get really lost. That's taking discomfort to a new level.

I traveled to Tanzania by myself in 2017, not knowing a single soul, to hike on Kilimanjaro. When I was one of 5 non-African people on a full plane on a connecting flight from Mombassa to Kilimanjaro, I embraced my status as an outsider and said in my mind, "Yes! Time to learn some new shit!" When the plane pulled up to a shoebox of an airport in Kilimanjaro in the stifling dry heat in late September and every foreign traveler stood in line for over an hour for a visa, my mind shifted again as I had to grow and learn despite my discomfort and frustration. When I finally stepped outside the shoebox to find a driver who was going to hold up my name card to get my attention and I couldn't find that person for 10 minutes, I had to make decisions in that searing hot weather – *do I wait some more because maybe they are running late? Do I call my travel company and let them know I don't see my driver? Do I scan all the name cards again because maybe my name is misspelled* (which happens a lot)?

When I checked into the hotel in Moshi that was more like a Super 8 Motel with 50-year-old faucets and bedsprings that had felt better days, I had to get over my first world expectations and count my blessings that I got to this vastly different continent safely and that I had enough time to rest before the 6-day hiking journey started the next day.

Growth happens when you come up to the plate batting against some curveballs, and traveling delivers some wonderfully gnarly curveballs. Love the growth and please, embrace the curveballs. You will become smarter and simply better for it.

You gradually get over this discomfort and all the newness, and foreign sights and sounds and ways become familiar. You learn the rules. You learn how to assert yourself with the limited vocabulary, using new words you pick up everyday. You learn to navigate in and out of this foreign place. You might be with a group, or maybe not. You learn shortcuts and best practices. You start to make sense of the system of the new land. You observe what works and what doesn't, and you oblige the customs that are reasonable within your moral compass.

But believe this: It's extraordinarily empowering to travel outside your locale, especially by yourself. It is nerve-wracking at first to learn everything, but it's an uplifting and phenomenal feeling to know you are overcoming obstacles and getting out of your comfort zone.

By last count I've traveled across twelve countries (grouping the French Polynesian islands and the Caribbean islands into two countries). I have learned a lot beyond getting from point A to B and how to say "thank you" in the local language. Traveling means I had to reach a level of humility to learn, to observe, to adapt and to blend in because what I knew in my head no longer applied as the norm or the custom in a foreign land. To do that successfully meant I had to grow as a person. Traveling has been a phenomenal vehicle to do that. For example, I learned that the Japanese and German respect for time in public transport are different from Americans'; and theirs is extraordinary, setting the bar "like clock work." I've seen an open farmers' market with cheerful vendors dressed in colorful garb in seemingly chill Moshi, Tanzania was only down the street from a convenience mart manned by armed security at the entrance. I have seen the juxtaposition of natural beauty and modern marvels at odds in Victoria Harbor of Hong Kong; so many tourist cameras and skyscrapers emasculate the gorgeousness of the harbor. I've learned that one city's idea of customer service in Japan is quite different from another metropolis when they are separated by only three hours train ride. I've seen that Denmark's love for bicycles is instilled early in their children and that bikes get their own traffic lights and lanes throughout Copenhagen which speaks enormously to other implications in the Danish society that we do not witness here in the States.

Nothing spectacular ever happens inside the comfort zone. Why would it, right? The same routine, day in and day out, hampers Learning and Growth from taking root and thriving. You cannot know what's different or interesting or better until you get out of your comfort zone and away from where everyone is doing the same thing, day after the day.

The first time I traveled outside my native country of Taiwan was at age 6 when my mother and I flew to Japan to spend winter with my uncle and his family. It was exciting and overwhelming to be on the plane for the first time and I had never seen so many wide freeway lanes traversing at the same time while my uncle's eggplant sedan took us to his suburban home (I named his car so due to its deep purple hue; the same car from which I nearly rolled out of and became a road-kill – see Travel Stories section in my book *You did WHAT now?!* for details). The efficiency and courtesy of Japanese city society was a marvel in and of itself; and that part still holds true when I made my second trip there in 2018 with my family.

The second time I traveled internationally was at age 11 and with different reasons. It was overwhelming, again, with a huge dose of trepidation because the flight from Taiwan to California was for a permanent move. Many of my extended family members – grandmother, the aunt and her family with whom my grandmother lived, another uncle plus several cousins were already in California. My mother wanted to escape my father and his scheming, gambling tendencies; so to protect her savings and us and to be closer to the rest of the family, she decided that it was best that we emigrate to the States. I cannot express how much growth I had from this particular travel and move – all of a sudden, I faced a new language and culture to learn, new friends-making skills to acquire, and just new EVERYTHING. When nothing you used to know was a sure thing anymore, you get serious growing pains and you have to learn to sink or swim, quickly. Although I resented my mother from robbing me from my comfort zone at the time – my friends, my elementary school where I was a straight A student and a popular kid, my city in which I had grown up – I am thankful for the experience to travel and live in a new country in which I was forced to grow up as a preadolescent and as a language learner.

Everything wonderful – new learning experiences, making new friendships, seeing new ways of doing things, witnessing different kinds of beauty that might inspire you – comes from getting outside of your box. The cool thing is that you can and should choose where you want to have these new, interesting experiences – by traveling. Erase township dividers and state lines; cross oceans and traverse continents. Do travel and allow your mind to become as big as the world.

This is why I travel to other cities in North America by myself a couple of times a year amid being a busy parent and author/speaker. This is why I flew by myself, at age twenty, from Los Angeles to New Orleans to attend my coed business fraternity's biannual conference shortly after being elected Chancellor of my chapter. I have attended lots of other events – some in town, some out of town – by myself since then. This is why I traveled to Tanzania by myself, not knowing a single soul, to hike on Kilimanjaro in 2017.

This is why I plan to travel to Nepal in 2019 to do another big bucket list hike. Whether I make the trip by my self or with people I know remains to be seen; but one thing is for sure – I will go to the places I want to go and I want the same for you.

By whatever means you can, travel outside of your city and out of your country. Get out of your well and see the beauty that is our world – which is a lot bigger than the fifty-mile radius the average person is used to.

Typical excuses I often hear when I encourage people to travel more is,

"Oh, but my husband/wife is so laid back and doesn't like to get out of our city."

"Oh, but I don't have any money to travel."

"Oh, I don't know if I could do this by myself."

To each of these, I say:

"Go by yourself or go with your own friends. You did things on your own before you met your spouse, right? You can do this on your own, too. And a little miss-you time never hurt anyone."

"Don't tell me you don't have money when I know you are dropping $4.50 at Starbucks on the daily. Save up the money for the trip you want to take. Maybe it means cutting some expenses, like your dang cell phone bill and your Starbucks addiction. It might take awhile but that's why we make a budget and a timeline, and we stick to it. Make your own damn Folgers coffee at home!"

"If you believe you can do it, then you can do it. You are whatever you believe you are."

Happy travels, my friends. Get out of town as I'd love to welcome you to the Badass Travelers Club to rejoice and hear all about your adventures!

Epilogue

I thank you for sticking with me up to the very end. My only goal in writing this book and having as many people as possible read it is to increase others' badassery. I hope to fuel your confidence, your pursuit of everything you want, in order to craft an amazing life that you desire. Know that this is not an overnight process. But the decision to turn on your inner badassery button takes but a moment because that's how long a decision takes. I know you can do it if you really want to.

Did you know I have a Badassery 101 course that you can do at your own pace? Yep. Just visit www. Roseanney.com click on Store, and download the course. It has six modules that teach you how to implement some steps I talked about here in this book.

I look forward to seeing your growth as a fellow badass. Find me on my social media below, anytime, and tell me what you think about the book. I would love to hear what resonated with you the most, and what you are starting to do to live out your badassery.

Go on now – be your best self and pursue life on your terms, and live out loud.

(f) : Write on, Roseanney

(⊙) : @roseanneyliu

(v) : @RoseanneyLiu

(www) : www.Roseanney.com

Download the freebie PDF today from my website and get 3 tips on how to start unleashing your badassery today.

Use this link and scroll to the bottom of the web-page: www.Roseanney.com

Acknowledgements

I have to thank my life experiences, first and foremost, without which I couldn't have had, lost, and then found my confidence – my inner badassery, which has carried me so far in accomplishing so many great things. Without life experiences – the ups and downs, the downright bizarre – life would be boring, and I wouldn't be accused of having a boring life, ever.

To my beta readers – Ann Johns Downey, George Foster, Alan Hall, Shahnaz Radji, and Gokatwemang Sololo - thank you for your feedback. You are a Godsend as every writer needs beta readers since we are so in our own heads with our work. I thank you for your honesty and suggestions in making *Badassery 101* better than its first drafts.

Of course, I have to thank my amazing copy editor, Elaine Ash, for putting up with me, a very rough manuscript, and my million-and-one questions. Elaine, I wouldn't be surprised if you needed a few drinks while editing this book but I'm glad you didn't because one of us needed to finesse sentences in a correct and coherent way.

I have had incredible support from my husband Daniel Getting and our kids Morgan and Jackson, whose support on my writing journey I hold dearly. Thank you for putting up with all my shit.

Last but not least, I thank you, friend and reader. I wrote this book for you because I want the best for you. Live the best life that you imagine possible because I know it is absolutely possible once you unleash your badassery. Don't worry if that inner confidence we were all born with might have gotten lost or muted along the way of Life. You can get it back, I promise. I want you to live out loud, to do everything you desire, and to be happy. Allow me to toast you on the journey to Badassery 101.

Also by Roseanney Liu

You did WHAT now?! (2017)
How to Survive Elementary School (2017)
Mastering Your Inner Game (collaboration, 2018)
Phenomenal Women (collaboration, 2018)